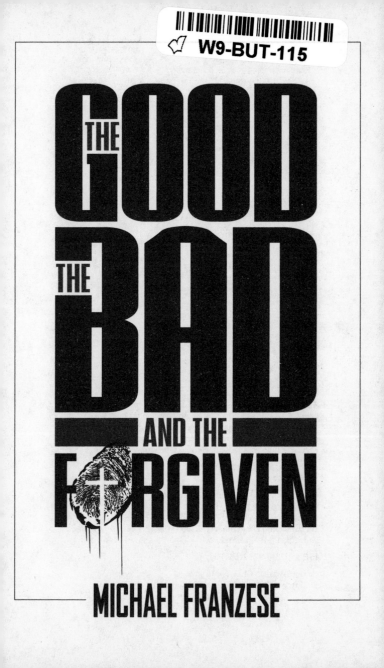

THE GOOD THE BAD AND THE FORGIVEN

MICHAEL FRANZESE

The Good, the Bad, and the Forgiven

Outreach, Inc., Vista, CA 92081
outreach.com

ISBN: 978-0-9787153-3-5

Cover artwork: Christen Bourgeois
Design and layout: Alexia Wuerdeman

IN MEMORY OF my two sisters,
Gia Marie and Cristina Marie Franzese.
May all of you who read these pages rejoice
with them in Heaven one day.

TABLE OF CONTENTS

TO THE READER,

The Merriam Webster Dictionary defines an accident as *an unforeseen and unplanned event or circumstance*. If you retrieved this book from the shelf and opened it to this page, the odds are it was not by accident. Even if you planned to do so after a moment's glance at the cover, it is not, by definition, an accident that you are reading these words.

It was most likely the title that caught your attention and prompted you to read beyond the cover. *The Good, the Bad, and the Forgiven*. Sounds like a title to a Western movie starring *the Good* guy, Clint Eastwood. Or perhaps it was the blurb on the back of the book about the "mob guy" that piqued your interest. Certainly, he must fall within the category of *the Bad* suggested by the title. Maybe it was neither or both of these that caused you to read further, or maybe the book fell off the shelf and hit you squarely on the head. Whatever the reason, I can almost assure you it is not by accident that you have this book in your hands at this moment.

Someone other then yours truly is trying to get your attention. I challenge you to read further. If you do, I just might make you an offer you cannot refuse.

[signature]

Michael Franzese

INTRODUCTION

*"For I know the plans I have
for you," declares the LORD,
"plans to prosper you and not
to harm you, plans to give you
hope and a future."*

—Jeremiah 29:11

I AM THE SON of one of the most feared crime bosses ever to walk the mobbed-up streets of Brooklyn, an enforcer known to be so cold-blooded and deadly that he evoked as much fear among his minions as the devil did among his. I'll never forget how Dad was once described in a 1965 news article entitled, "The Hood in Our Neighborhood":

*John (Sonny) Franzese, 45…tabbed as
the fastest rising young executive in the
Cosa Nostra empire of crime. His business:
supervision of underworld rackets in parts
of Brooklyn, Manhattan and Queens and in
almost all of Nassau and Suffolk counties.
The tools of his trade: greed, fear and, when
necessary, the gun.*
　　　　　　　　　　　　　—Long Island's *Newsday*, 1965

*(Author's note: Unsubstantiated claims by law
enforcement officials say that as many as
thirty-five unfortunate mobsters were victims
of the latter.)*

La Cosa Nostra means "this thing of ours" in Italian. The LCN, as it is known by the FBI, can best be described as an organization comprised of different "families" whose members are linked by blood ties and who engage in various forms of organized criminal activities. It is more commonly known as the Mafia. Its "made" members refer to it simply as "the life."

I chose to follow Dad's infamous footsteps into the life, and I would soon prove to be as lethal in the skyscrapers of the business world as my father had been on the streets of New York. My area of criminal expertise differed from that of my father's, but I was definitely a mobster, heavily entrenched in the business of organized crime.

*Within a decade, Franzese had become…
one of the biggest earners the mob had seen
since Capone, and the youngest individual in
Fortune magazine's survey of "The 50 Biggest
Mafia Bosses."*
—Vanity Fair, February 1991

*The biggest problem we encountered was
that…Michael had so much going on—car
dealerships, bank loans, money laundering,
unions, gas taxes, gas terminals, insurance
fraud, counterfeit bonds, loan-sharking and
gambling operations, construction businesses,
movies, the Russians, you name it…*
—Ray Jermyn, assistant U.S. district attorney

Those were my business activities during
the almost twenty years I spent as a member
of La Cosa Nostra. But that was then. I do
not consider myself a mobster any longer.
I defected from that life over a decade ago.
The circumstances of my defection were
difficult; the mob doesn't let one of its own
just walk away. There is no retirement age. I
did not sign a contract upon my induction.
There is no out-clause, no "take this job and
shove it" when a made man wants out. Much
of what I know about the secret life remains
locked inside my mind and my heart. The
oath demands that once you're in, you are
in for life. You either leave in a coffin, or you
cooperate with the government and enter

the Witness Protection Program. Yet I have done neither.

> *There's an old saying that the only way to leave the Mafia is in a coffin. Members are pledged to a lifetime of secrecy, and to quit would be to arouse suspicion that you are cooperating with the police or federal agents. Such breaches of faith are punishable with death.*
>
> —*Life* magazine, December 1967

My defection from the life resulted in years of struggles for myself and my wife and children: a mob contract on my life, a period of total alienation from my father and most of my blood relatives, intense government pressure to become a cooperating witness. It was all part of the price I paid for my defection from the Colombo crime family. Experts on both sides of the law predicted I would end up dead, like all the others before me who had violated the secret code in one way or another.

> *I wouldn't want to be in Michael Franzese's shoes. I don't think his life expectancy is very substantial.*
>
> —Edward McDonald, former attorney-in-charge Organized Crime/Strike Force Eastern District of New York, 1991

He will get whacked!
—Bernie Welsh, former FBI agent, 1991

But I am very much alive today—at least I was at the time of this writing—and I believe I know why. Some people in government would have you believe that I bought off the soldiers who were given the contract to whack me. Others theorized I paid the family boss ten million dollars to spare my life. If the officials who arrived at those conclusions really understood the life, they would know those theories are preposterous. The mob would have taken my money all right, and then would have killed me anyway. They don't honor deals with defectors.

There are still others in law enforcement who believe I never really left the mob—that I am still somehow secretly involved in the life. With all the informants and high-tech surveillance equipment used to investigate the mob today, there are very few secrets remaining from law enforcement. For me to have somehow managed to remain in the life undetected for a number of years is, quite simply, absurd.

I'm alive today because I serve a different boss—a boss whose plan for my life did not call for my execution at the hands of a Mafia assassin. And when *this* boss has a plan, no one and nothing will stand in the way of his plan being fulfilled—not even a vengeful mobster packing a pistol and a pair of cement shoes.

As a sworn member of La Cosa Nostra through a multitude of arrests, indictments and years in prison, I experienced first-hand the proverbial *long arm of the law*. As a believer in Jesus Christ, I am blessed to have experienced the even *longer arm of the Lord*. A loving God reached into the depths of the underworld to rescue a Mafia soldier. His arms extended unscathed through the razor-wired fences and cold steel doors of a prison cell to give me comfort and peace at a most dire time in my life. He will reach into the devil's own worldly cauldrons to rescue even the most hard-core sinner and the most long-lost soul. No one is beyond His mighty reach.

I have been given a new purpose in life: *to share what God has done for me* with all of you who feel you are too bad a person, too unworthy of God's saving grace or in far too hopeless a situation to ever fulfill His purpose in your own life. If God will save a notorious Mafia caporegime (captain) with blood-stained hands and have a plan and purpose for his life, then **NO ONE** is so bad that they are beyond the reach of God's infinite love and mercy.

> *"Though your sins are like scarlet, they shall be as white as snow; though they are red as crimson, they shall be like wool."*
>
> —Isaiah 1:18

NO ONE is left out of the plan that God has for all of our lives.

> *"For I know the plans I have for you,"* declares the Lord, *"plans to prosper you and not to harm you, plans to give you hope and a future."*
>
> —Jeremiah 29:11

NO ONE is beneath or beyond fulfilling God's purpose in their life.

> *So do not be ashamed to testify about our Lord...who has saved us and called us to a holy life—not because of anything we have done but because of His own purpose and grace...*
>
> —2 Timothy 1:8, 9

My life is a mob story, but it's also a love story. It tells of a young boy's love for his father—a love that bound him by blood to the underworld of the Mafia, until an innocent young woman walked into his life. Her exotic beauty captivated him. Her faith in God saved him. His love of God protected him.

In the pages that follow, I invite you to come along with me as I tell you how God took me through a life-long process of revealing His plan for my life and preparing me to fulfill that purpose.

CHAPTER 1:
THE FAMILY

*"...I gave you my solemn oath and
entered into a covenant with you,
declares the Sovereign LORD,
and you became mine."*

—Ezekiel 16:8

CRISTINA CAPOBIANCO WAS a beautiful,
seventeen-year-old telephone operator who
moonlighted as a hat-check girl and rov-
ing photographer at a ritzy Manhattan
restaurant known as The Stork Club. In the
early 1950s, the exclusive night spot had a
four-star celebrity clientele that included
the likes of Marilyn Monroe, Grace Kelly,

Damon Runyon, and super-journalist and broadcaster Walter Winchell. It was also a favorite spot of some of the city's most infamous mobsters, among them the Colombo family's rising star, Sonny Franzese.

Cristina was a pet of club owner Sherman Billingsley and a special favorite of frequent club guest Montgomery Clift, the dashing young movie star who was often linked in the tabloids to Elizabeth Taylor. But Cristina's relationships mattered little to my pop once she caught his eye. He made his move and quickly replaced Clift, who was not about to butt heads with a notorious killer over a hat-check girl. The actor was smart enough to realize that in real life, the good guy doesn't always get the girl.

Dad and Mom fell in love and, the way they tell it, capped a whirlwind courtship by tying the knot on July 24, 1951, one day after her eighteenth birthday. At thirty-two, Dad was quite a bit her senior. Regardless, they became "The Mobster and the Hat-Check Girl." Their love affair might have made good fodder for a made-for-television movie, had there been such a thing back then.

There was, however, a slight wrinkle in their fantasy romance. Dad was married once before, to an attractive German woman named Ann Schiller. The marriage was said to have been rocky from the start, and it ended in divorce a few years after their third child was born. And, as young as she was, Mom had also been married before. At sixteen, she hooked up with a handsome young soldier named Louis Grillo, and their teenage love affair, although it barely survived a year, had produced none other than yours truly—me. I was Louis Grillo's son by birth, but as far back as I can remember, Sonny Franzese accepted me as his own. He was, therefore, the only dad I ever really knew.

As it turned out, Mom was obliged to return the favor three times over when, shortly after their wedding day, Dad took custody of his three children and our household increased overnight to a family of six. Within a few short years, Mom and Dad would produce three more children, and by 1965 our family was one sibling up on the Brady Bunch. But further comparisons to that joyful brood would end with the numbers. Ours was not one big happy family. Although Dad accepted me as his own, Mom had a lot more difficulty accepting his children. The blended household had been a heated issue between Mom and Dad from the start. At the ripe age of eighteen, Mom wasn't ready to be a mother of four. She felt Dad's kids belonged with their mother, and she was not shy about letting him know it. But Ann Schiller wasn't cooperating in that regard and, as a result, my step-siblings were the subject of many heated arguments. I can recall one such ugly confrontation when I arrived home from school on a cold and snowy winter afternoon.

"What am I supposed to do, throw them out in the streets?" I heard my father shout. "My hands are tied!" My eyes widened as I saw my ten-year-old stepbrother, Carmine, wander through the battleground on his way to the refrigerator. He appeared oblivious to the shouting, having heard this argument a hundred times before. Mom momentarily interrupted her ranting and grabbed the barefoot Carmine. Apparently, she was really determined to make her point with Dad this time, because she then proceeded to escort him out the front door and toss him into the yard, which was full of freshly fallen snow.

I was stunned. I immediately ran to the window and saw my stepbrother hopping up and down on the ice and freezing snow. My mother had never gone this far before. A wave of terror shot through me. I figured

Dad would be so outraged at what Mom had done, he would surely take his anger out on me.

My mind was racing. I wasn't about to be thrown out in the snow by my father because of my mother's actions. I rushed over to her and tugged at her waist. "Stop!" I cried. "Why did you do that to Carmine? Let him in!" I wanted Dad to know I didn't agree with Mom's treatment of his son. But deep inside, I was mostly worried that Dad might turn on me one day because of how Mom treated his children. Of the seven children in our house, I was the only one who didn't have Sonny Franzese's blood running through his veins. If my mother wanted my father's previous children out of the house, what would happen when Dad decided to go *quid pro quo*? I had expressed this concern to my mom on several occasions. Her assurances that my place in the house was secure did little to ease my anxiety.

In fairness to Mom, it must have been difficult for a newlywed eighteen-year-old to wake up one morning and learn she was now the mother to three young children. At the time, I was too young to understand her dilemma. The issue over my step-siblings continued to be a flash point between my parents, and I grew so nervous over it that at one point I tried to run away and live with my grandparents. I grew up wanting nothing more than to *belong* to my family, to *belong* with my dad. I didn't want to be there if my father, whom I absolutely idolized, finally turned on me.

But no matter how coolly Mom treated my stepbrother and sisters, Dad never gave me reason for concern. He never withdrew an ounce of love from me. He always made me feel I belonged. And I never forgot.

My single-minded desire became to please my dad in every way. He was adamant about my education. He would lecture me, "Ya gotta go to school, son. Without an education, you're going nowhere in life." So, to please him, I brought home straight As.

I was an athlete and played three sports in school. Dad wanted me to be the best, so he spent time schooling me in athletics. During the summer months, he taught me how to hit and catch a baseball by playing Pepper in the backyard. When I went on to play Little League baseball, my dad would never miss a game. He would arrive at the field in a black Cadillac, sharply dressed in a dark suit and always in the company of a few of his men. Dad and his crew were always the center of attention as they walked to the stands to watch me play. If I was ever up to bat when Dad arrived, the umpire would take one look at him and never call strike three on me. I quickly found out that it's good to have a dad in the mob when you play sports.

When the weather cooled, we would put away the bats and gloves and bring out the Joe Namath football. Dad was a firm but encouraging taskmaster, ordering me to always put forth a maximum effort, even in practice. He would tell me, "You have talent, son. Don't ever let me see you waste it."

In the backyard of my mom's parents' house, Dad and I created a game called Off the Wall. We would bounce a pink rubber ball off the chimney and try to catch the rebound before it hit the ground. A catch was worth a point. Hitting the ledge where the cement base merged with the red brick chimney and catching it on a fly was worth five points. The first one to hit five hundred points won. We would play for hours at a time.

As I entered my teens, the game became fiercely competitive. We were pretty evenly matched, and we each hated to lose. If Dad fell behind, I had to watch him closely to make sure he didn't inflate his score or try to shave points from mine. (Dad liked to cheat.) We would argue and laugh and toss that ball until it was too dark to see the rebounds.

The backyard contests and training sessions went on for more than a decade. As busy as he was, Dad always made time to play with me. In my eyes, he was the world's greatest father, and I cherished every minute we spent together. As the years passed, my insecurity over being a stepchild eased. Nothing was ever said between us, but my father's unqualified acceptance of me as his son made an indelible impression on this young boy, and an even greater impression on the man I would one day become.

My father's downfall began in 1964, when a series of arrests and charges brought against him by both state and federal prosecutors would eventually land him behind bars for a very long time. He was charged in three separate indictments for murder, grand larceny, and conspiracy to commit bank robbery. Although the state charges ended in Dad's acquittal after two lengthy trials, his federal trial in 1967 ended in a conviction for masterminding a nationwide string of bank robberies.

I was devastated when Dad was hauled off to prison, and in the fall of 1972 it led to me making a dramatic career change. Enrolled as a pre-med student at Long Island's Hofstra University, I dropped out of college in order to focus on springing my dad from what could become a lifetime behind bars. My mom was leading the charge to prove Dad's innocence, doing the best a mother of four could do in a war against the all-powerful Justice Department.

Freeing him would be no easy task for me, either. I would have to track down the witnesses who framed him and get them to recant their perjured testimony. They were four admitted drug addicts who concocted a story and peddled it to the Feds in exchange for a get-out-of-jail card. The sorry quartet went on a nationwide bank robbery spree and, thanks to a lame defense orchestrated by my old man's lawyer, they got a jury to believe my pop was the mastermind behind their scheme. The Honorable Judge Jacob Mishler sealed the deal, hitting Dad with fifty big ones and ordering him carted off to Leavenworth. It was a frame-up of epic proportions. For me to have even a shot at proving Dad's innocence, I needed to level the playing field. I would need to have "juice" on the streets, and money—lots of money!

To achieve this, my father proposed me for membership into the Colombo family. "If you are going to be on the streets, you need to be on the streets the right way," I remember him saying to me while I was visiting him at the penitentiary. He sent a message to the family in Brooklyn, and soon after I was summoned to a meeting with the family boss, Tom DiBella. "From now on, La Cosa Nostra comes before anything and everything in your life," he instructed me. "And that means, if your mother is sick and she's dying and this family calls you to service, you leave your mother's side and come to serve this family. When and if we feel that you have proven yourself worthy to become a member, we will let you know." These were ominous words delivered by a powerful man who presided over a very powerful mob family, a family into which I was now formally proposed for adoption.

Most people believe that the mob is a business. Make no mistake, the mob is more than a business; it is a way of life. La Cosa Nostra is a sub-culture of society with its own set of rules and policies. It operates under a moral framework that is Machiavellian at its core. It impacts the lives of all those who come in contact with its sworn members. For most, the results are far from desirable and often they are devastating.

For nearly a year after meeting with Di-Bella, I was engaged in the mob's version of boot camp. The family took this time to train its "recruits" in discipline, carefully measuring their character and indoctrinating them into the mob life. Only a few months earlier, I had been a student majoring in biology on the campus of a university. Now, I was getting my master's degree in the business of the mob. It was a major career change for sure, but one I was able to make to the satisfaction of the family's hierarchy.

The moment of my formal induction into the mob came on Halloween night, 1975. I was one of six recruits to be inducted that evening at a secret location in the mob's stronghold of Brooklyn. Each of us was individually called into a room. The lights were dim, and the mood in the room was as solemn as the darkness. In the center of the room, the hierarchy of the Colombo family sat on folding chairs arranged in a U-shape. As I walked inside the U, I recognized the stern faces of the men sitting around me. The captains were on the edges—the closer a man sat to the center, the more powerful his position. In the exact middle of the U was the boss, Tom DiBella. The seats to his left and right were reserved for the family's underboss and consigliere.

I stood in front of DiBella.

"Are you ready to take the oath of La Cosa Nostra?" the big man asked.

"Yes," I answered.

"Then, cup your hands."

I did as I was ordered, and a Catholic altar card with a picture of a saint appeared in DiBella's hand. He dropped it into the pocket formed by my hands and lit it aflame.

"Tonight, Michael Franzese, you are born again into a new life, La Cosa Nostra," he said as the saint burned in my hands. "And if you violate this oath, if you betray your brothers, then you will die and burn in hell like this saint is burning in your hands."

I felt only a tinge of heat as the saint was quickly consumed. The act was purely symbolic—not, as some believe, a show of toughness or of the ability to withstand pain.

DiBella grabbed my hand, cut my finger and squeezed it tightly as drops of my blood splattered on the floor. "This oath is sealed with your blood," he intoned. "Should you violate this oath, your blood will be shed."

That's how it began for me. I now belonged to a new family—bound by blood to the underworld of La Cosa Nostra. My purpose in joining the life was clear. I was motivated to do two things: to get my dad out of prison, and to make money. In the mob, not unlike the real world, money leads to power, and that power would give me the "juice" I needed to help spring my father.

Suffice to say, I wasted no time in garnering noteworthy success in pursuit of those goals. Dad was really proud of me as I quickly rose through the mob ranks, generating money from the streets in the way that Michael Milken was generating money from his junk bonds. Back then my dad and I—the mob's elder statesman and its young rising star—were quite the team to be reckoned with.

My father had a clear-cut agenda in bringing me into the life. Had the Feds not derailed his infamous career with that phony bank robbery rap, Dad would have become the boss—godfather of the Colombo family. And if I listened to him once I joined the ranks, I would take his rightful place on the family's throne. Dad would guide me through the treacherous maze of mob politics and ultimately land me in the top seat. I would one day be the head of the Colombo crime family.

CHAPTER 2:

THE HUNTED

They have tracked me down,
they now surround me, with eyes
alert, to throw me to the ground.

—Psalm 17:11

MY OPERATION WAS generating an enormous amount of money, which in turn resulted in the rapid expansion of my crew. I controlled a couple hundred men, including a tough group of Russians from Brighton Beach, Brooklyn. My business operations, legitimate and illegitimate, had grown and diversified, and one of them was particularly lucrative. For close to a decade, I had masterminded a scheme to defraud Uncle Sam out of a few billion dollars in gasoline tax money—a cool thirty-five cents per gallon. It was this racket that eventually became the focus of the Feds' attention and their desire for vengeance.

> At this point, the money pouring into the Franzese/Iorizzo operation started resembling the Gross National Product of a mid-sized country. Conservative estimates have Michael and the Fat Man personally making between $5 million and $8 million a week for nearly three years...

> Michael's power inside the New York Mafia families grew with every dollar. His legend outside the Mafia grew even larger. A deputy attorney general in the United States Department of Justice reported to a congressional subcommittee that Michael's operation had grown so large that he had been awarded his own Long Island-based family and had jumped from being a Colombo captain to a full-fledged, Marlon Brando-like Mafia don. That was an exaggeration; the Colombo family wasn't about to allow their golden goose to escape. Still, it's not hard to see how the Feds got that impression...[1]

---

[1] From Dary Matera, *Quitting the Mob*, HarperCollins, 1991. Lawrence Iorizzo, "The Fat Man," was Michael's main business associate in the gasoline scam. He later cooperated with the government in proseccutions against Michael and others.

By the age of thirty-four, I was on a fast-track to have more battles with the government then many mob guys have in a lifetime. It all came to a head on a spring day in 1983. On April 21, law enforcement officials from eleven different state, county, and federal organizations gathered as a massive task force, presided over by Ed McDonald, Organized Crime Strike Force Chief for the Eastern District of New York. They came together with a single, crucial assignment—bring down the "Prince of the Mafia." That morning, the newly formed task force met in the basement of the federal courthouse in Uniondale, New Jersey, clothed in stiff suits and burning with ambition to break a young, financially powerful superstar of the mob. Over the next year, they would spend thirty-six full days meeting together and crafting their plan for justice and retribution.

The Organized Crime Strike Force, along with other law enforcement agencies, had a bull's eye on my back for years, and they were building an air-tight case against me even as I worked my plan to accumulate wealth and spring my dad. But these weren't the only legal opponents I would have to face. Across the river in Manhattan, my underworld activities had come to the attention of yet another formidable G-Man: Rudolph Giuliani, the illustrious United States attorney for the Southern District of New York. He and his team of racket-busting law men were preparing to upstage the task force and slam me with charges of their own. In the fall of 1984, I was charged, along with fifteen other associates, in an overwhelming twenty-nine count racketeering indictment.

The federal courthouse in Manhattan was the scene of my first federal trial. I had been tried four times previously by the State of New York and had won every case, but the Feds were different. I had fought them for years on my dad's behalf and knew them as formidable opponents. I was charged with violations of the Racketeer Influenced and Corrupt Organizations Act (RICO), and RICO cases were notoriously difficult to defend. For sure, this would be a tough one to beat, and Giuliani was a tough prosecutor. To make matters worse, Giuliani had a personal agenda. He was determined to jail every alleged mobster whose criminal behavior (in his view) had sullied the name of decent, law-abiding Italian-Americans— himself included. My conviction would likely result in my spending the rest of my natural life in a federal prison cell.

The trial began in January 1984 and lasted for several months. The weeks prior to and during the trial were extremely stressful for me. A trip to my internist confirmed what the burning in my chest had been signaling for months—I had a duodenal ulcer. Even though I felt the trial was going my way, I knew that one can never be sure of the outcome when a case goes to the jury. Juries are unpredictable, even fickle at times, and those few seconds between the judge's order for the defendant to "rise and face the jury" and the jury delivering its verdict are among the most intense moments one can experience. Weak knees, clenched jaw, sweaty palms, and heart palpitations accompany the prayer that pleads for God to have one simple word leave the jury foreman's lips before the judgment word of guilty: "Not!" That one simple word can, in an instant, dramatically change the course of a person's life.

But something happened before the end of the trial that, for a few harrowing hours, made even that pending verdict seem insignificant. It caused me, for the first time in my life, to openly challenge my father, the man who had been my hero since childhood, the man that I loved and admired more than any other man on earth.

CHAPTER 3:
THE CODE

There is a way that seems right to a man, but in the end it leads to death.

—Proverbs 14:12

IT STARTED WITH a call from my fellow mob caporegime, Vincent "Jimmy" Angellino, a close friend who had been among the five men inducted into the family along with me.

"The Boss wants you to come in for a meeting late tonight."

"What's this about?" I asked, dreading the answer.

"The Boss wants you in," was all he would say.

But his voice was as lifeless as I had ever heard it, and I knew Jimmy well. I immediately called my father who, as a result of the effort put forth by my mother and myself, was free on parole from his fifty-year federal prison term. As I expected, he had just received a similar call, but his "sit-down" was scheduled for a few hours earlier than mine.

"We need to talk, Dad," I said. "I'll be right over."

"No, I'll come there," he said.

As I waited for Dad in my home in Brookville, Long Island, I thought about what could have prompted the meetings. My operation had brought me a steady diet of notoriety, and it was making my mob associates very uncomfortable. There was talk within mob circles—inflamed by the federal government and local news reports—that my crew had become so powerful that I had broken away from the Colombo crime family and become the boss of my own family. At the heart of these rumors was the mistaken belief that I was making more money than I was turning in to my boss in Brooklyn and was holding back millions of dollars.

Angellino's call now confirmed my worst fears: I was in serious trouble. And because my father would defend me to the death, mob policy dictated that he too was in serious trouble. It was that Machiavellian philosophy the mob lived under: "The ruler must determine all injuries that he will need to inflict. He must inflict them once and for all." We both knew about these meetings; they were a part of the life. You walk into a meeting like that, and you never walk out again.

It was this perception that was fueling my irritation. Instead of Dad and me banding together and going out in a blaze of gunfire, I knew he would want us to walk into that room at our scheduled times, like lambs to the slaughter, and passively accept whatever fate awaited us. Of all the aspects of the mob life I had grown to despise, the legendary death summons was the worst. I had long ago vowed never to walk into a room where someone was waiting to take my life.

As I impatiently waited for my father that evening, I realized we were about to engage in a verbal life-or-death struggle that would pit the old mob values of strict adherence to the code against the saner interpretation held by the second generation of mobsters, myself included. I wondered what argument Dad would use to support his position, beyond blind military-like allegiance. His methods had brought nothing but decades of grief, hardship, and heartache to himself and his family.

When Dad arrived, I met him in the driveway. It was late afternoon, and the air was a bit chilly for a spring day. As the sun set, I was reminded of that game of ball my dad and I would play in my grandfather's backyard, each of us fiercely determined to claim victory over the other.

"I have a bad feeling about this, Dad. I don't like it. You in first and then me...this isn't right."

"Son, this is our life. We've been given an order, and we must obey."

"Dad, do you hear what you're saying? Do you understand what's going on here? What about our lives? What about our family and the people who rely on us? Aren't they more important than our oath? All of this is over money. You know the rumors out there. So now they're calling us in, and you know what's going to happen."

"I don't think so," he said.

"Neither one of us is sure, though," I said, "so why should we do this? Why risk our lives?"

He answered simply, "This is our way. Whatever happens tonight—happens."

This shook me, and I responded in a stern voice, "Are you kidding me?"

For a moment, Dad was shocked. I had never taken that tone with him, and the air was suddenly silent. He just stood there like a rock, saying nothing, feeling nothing, determined to live by the code right to the end.

"Okay, Dad. Okay. I know how you are. I know this is our life and we believe in it. I know what the oath demands; if they call us, we drop everything and go. Okay. But let's go together. Me and you, together! We shouldn't let anyone or anything separate us."

"We can't do that," he said. "That's not how the boss wants it. We can't change it, and we can't show fear."

"Fear? Is that what this is about? Showing fear? You're going to walk in there and let them stick a gun to the back of your head and blow your brains out so you won't be accused by some punk of showing fear? You're going to let them kill me, your son, just because you don't want to show fear?"

"This is the life we chose," he repeated. "We took an oath to honor this life. The boss gives an order, we obey that order. That's it."

"Even if it means we lose our lives over some phony rumors? What are you thinking, Dad? I'm all about honoring the oath I took, but I'm also about having a fighting chance to defend myself. I always envisioned it would be me and you, side by side, if we ever got the call. Me and you, back to back, blasting our way to the top or going down like warriors. Where is the fear in that? If we're going to die tonight, let's do it that way. Let's go out together, fighting."

He looked away from me and shook his head. My argument was falling on deaf ears. My adrenaline must have been peaking, because I did something I never thought I would do to my father. I grabbed him by the shoulders and forced him to look me in the eye. I could feel the power in his body swell as he turned and faced me. Dad was a powerful man, and he wasn't used to being manhandled. I could tell his instinct was to break free from my grasp. His eyes burned into mine with an intensity that was known to bring men to their knees.

"Dad, listen to me," I pleaded. "Let's go together." He stared at me for a few moments as I felt the tension begin to drain from his body.

"That's not our way, son," he repeated. "We will go in separately, the way we were ordered. I will obey the oath I took. I advise you to do the same. Whatever happens tonight—happens."

He walked to his car and opened the door. "It's the right thing, Michael," he said, standing there with the door open. "I believe it will be okay. If you have done nothing wrong, we have nothing to worry about. But if not, we live by the oath. We die by the oath." As he got into his car, he turned to me once more. "Know that I love you, son." With that, he drove off and disappeared into the night.

I paced the driveway, and then I walked around the grounds of my home. My senses were even more intense than before, but now I was desperately trying to make sense of the primal signals my body was sending out. Maybe I was overreacting. Maybe my father was bravely following his beliefs because he knew something I didn't. Surely he wouldn't place his own son at risk. Or maybe he knew that he wasn't the one on the spot, that he could disavow any detailed knowledge of my operation. I had intentionally kept him at a distance to protect him from a parole violation. Now he could use that distance to his advantage.

But wait a minute, I thought. *This is my father. We're as close as a father and son could be—sharing an even closer bond between a father and son because of the blood oath we took. Why am I questioning his judgment? Surely he would not place me in harm's way. He would sacrifice himself before he would let anything or anyone hurt me. This is the same man who never turned on me when I was a child. Why would he do so now?*

The time drew near, and I had no clearer answer than before. I was sure that I should not go, but if I failed to show, I could be sentencing my father to death. This was the mob way, and therein lay my answer. I got into my car and drove to Brooklyn.

CHAPTER 4:
THE MEETING

Even my close friend, whom
I trusted, he who shared my bread,
has lifted up his heel against me.

—Psalm 41:9

PARKING ON THE STREET, I walked to the café where Jimmy Angellino was scheduled to pick me up. I hadn't been told where the meeting was taking place, but this was typical. Instead of being allowed to drive there myself, I would be driven to the meeting location by another family member.

Jimmy was cold and distant as we drove, engaging only in small talk about the New

York Yankees. I'm a die-hard Yankee fan, but I wasn't interested in baseball that night. Jimmy and I had been "made" together and remained close friends over the years. I felt shaky and empty inside, but I fought the urge to question him about what lay ahead. I guess deep down, like my dad, I didn't want to show fear.

We drove in silence for about ten minutes. Then Jimmy pulled up to a large, dark house in Brooklyn, a house I had never seen before. *What a perfect place for a hit,* I thought. I expected the "meet" would be held downstairs in a soundproof basement. We exited the car, and Jimmy directed me to a path that led to the basement door. I walked slowly in front and Jimmy followed close behind.

When I entered the house, I would face either of two possibilities. If I opened the door and found the room empty, I was dead the moment I set foot in the room. I'd be clocked before I could turn my head. On the other hand, if there were people in the room, it might mean they were giving me the respect of a hearing first. In that situation, I expected to see acting-boss Andrew Russo (Carmine "the Snake" Persico, the Colombo family boss, was in jail) and the entire family hierarchy seated around a table. A young mob soldier, a recruit ready to earn his stripes, would be stationed by my side, but set back so I couldn't see him if he got up. That man would be my assassin. One nod from Russo, and I would be a dead man.

As I walked, I wondered, *Is Jimmy following behind me for a reason? Is he even now pulling the revolver from his waistband?*

My senses had suddenly become so sharp, so pumped with adrenaline, that the whole world looked different. This feeling was different than the one I experienced when facing a jury. Colors were brighter, sounds and smells more intense. I could see everything around me in greater detail. It was as if my entire body was powering up for a fight to the death.

I continued down the path leading to a narrow stairway; at the bottom was the basement door. My senses were so heightened that, even in the pitch-black of the night, I could see and smell the vividly colored flowers lining the pathway. The sound of a cricket chirping in the night was like a thousand drums beating in my ears. Fireflies appeared like patrol car lights flashing warning signals of impending danger.

I reached the foot of the stairs. My heart was beating so fast, I could almost feel it protruding through my chest. *Would the last image I'd see on this earth be whatever confronted me on the other side of that door?* I would have gladly traded my place at that doorstep for a seat at the defendant's table, even if I did not hear the word "Not" before the jury rendered its verdict. I could appeal a guilty verdict, but there's no appeal for a gunshot blast to the back of your head.

What had made me get in that car, walk down that path and stand at the precipice of what might be my entrance to eternity? Surely my eternity would be in hell. I was a criminal, a mobster who had lived every day of his mob life in violation of the laws of God and man. Yet in spite of that, I asked God to spare me as I stood at that doorstep, to let me live to see another day. *Isn't it ironic,* I wondered, *how in moments like this we turn to our Creator for mercy, even when we know we deserve none?*

The door swung open. I took a deep breath. On shaky knees, I slowly stepped inside, doing my best to put up a brave front. *I would show no fear. Accept my fate like a man. Do my father proud.*

As I entered the room, my mind went blank. My eyes perceived nothing but a pale shade of gray. The silence I experienced for that brief moment was deafening. I felt numb, as if my senses shut down as some kind of protective measure, so that whatever was to happen would be a blur, a dream. For that very brief moment I was in a trance-like state, oblivious to sight, sound, or touch.

Then there was a voice, then more voices, images, sounds, and smells. There were people in the room. In a fraction of a second, my senses roared back and became razor-sharp. Instantly, I took in my surroundings. I found everything exactly as I envisioned it; it was as if I had seen that table, those men, and maybe my death in forgotten dreams. Curiously, my father was nowhere in the room. *What did that mean? Was his absence meant as a message to me? Was I to assume the worst?*

The assassin was also just as I imagined: a young, hard-looking man sitting alone at the closest end of the table. He was a recruit, all right, one I had not yet met and maybe never would. By the end of the night, I might even become his ticket for entrance into the Colombo crime family. I noticed a bead of sweat forming on his temple. Russo had been my first caporegime when I had been a young soldier myself. He would give the signal, and I knew that whatever it was, no matter how secret or cloaked Russo tried to make it, I would recognize it as clear as a flashing billboard. It would be my last thought.

"We want to ask you about your business," Russo opened as I sat down in the chair to his right.

"Go ahead," I said.

For the next two hours, Russo and the other family capos grilled me on every aspect of my operation. But I was now in my element. I knew the life well, having learned from the best: my father—my hero. I answered them firmly in a strong, unwavering voice. I knew that if I couldn't go out shooting, I could certainly compete with my contemporaries in a war of wits. They wouldn't get the best of me there. "Ask me all your questions," I told them. "I have done nothing wrong."

Each of the men took turns peppering me with questions, attempting to trap me into revealing the whereabouts of the hidden millions that had been the subject of all those rumors. They even tried to trap me into saying something that didn't match my father's story. But I had expected that move and was well-prepared to defeat the tactic.

The intensity of the questioning was reaching a crescendo when Russo finally did give a signal, but it wasn't the signal I had earlier expected. Instead, Russo motioned for someone to serve the wine. My explanation had been accepted, at least for this night. I turned and subtly glanced at my designated assassin. He was slowly wiping the beads of sweat from his forehead.

The wine tasted sharp and bitter. My body had been on such a razor's edge that it seemed to alter my internal chemistry. My "brothers" walked around the room, chatted with me and talked among themselves. It was as if nothing had happened, as if everything was back to normal. But I couldn't focus on their words. Just moments before, they had been about to sentence me to death. I would never forget it, and it would never be the same for me, not with this "family" or my own.

I said goodnight to Andrew and all of my fellow capos. As we shook hands and exchanged the mob's customary kiss on the cheek, my mind suddenly flashed to an image from my childhood days as an altar boy in St. Anne's Church. It was the Biblical scene in which Judas betrayed Jesus to His accusers, His assassins, with a kiss on the cheek. And there I was, among a roomful of would-be betrayers, exchanging a kiss on the cheek with all of them. Jesus was innocent, wrongly accused by a man He had eaten dinner with the night before, betrayed by a man He had truly loved, betrayed by a man who had claimed to love Him. I had been wrongly accused on that night by some of my brothers in La Cosa Nostra. For those few moments, it made me sick to my stomach to be among them, but it made me even sicker to realize I was one of them. I would have done the same thing if I had been in their position; it was the way things worked in the mob. I was no better than anyone in that room and maybe worse.

"Jimmy, if they were going to whack me tonight, if the decision had been made, would you have told me?" I asked as he drove me back to my car.

He glanced at me for a moment. "Had it been the other way around, Michael, if I had been in your position tonight, would you have warned me?" he countered.

I pondered his question for a few seconds.

"No," I admitted. "That's sick, isn't it, Jimmy? We've known each other most all of our lives. What kind of friends are we? What kind of life is this?"

"It's our life, Michael, the life we chose. We knew what we were getting into when we took the oath, you above all. You've lived with it from the day you were born."

That was true. Who understood the life better than me? Tonight my father had acted just as anyone would have predicted—in blind adherence to the oath. Or did he? I still couldn't help but think there was something strange about his reaction to all of this.

"I tell ya something, Michael," Jimmy said. "You handled yourself well in there tonight. You were ice, man. You sat in the car like I was taking you to dinner."

"Looks can be deceiving," I answered. "My heart was pounding."

We arrived back at the café, and before I got out of the car, Jimmy made an unexpected confession. "I wouldn't have told you if you were a dead man tonight, but I can tell you now. You had a serious problem going in, both you and your father. You somehow talked your way out of it. It was a brilliant performance."

I thanked him for the accolades and was getting out of the car when he reached over, grabbed my arm, and whispered, "I'm going to tell you something, Michael, that you are not going to want to hear. This stays between you and me. Do I have your word on that?"

"Of course," I replied, having no idea what could be such a monumental revelation.

His hand tightly gripping my arm, Jimmy looked me dead in the eye. "Your father did not help you in there tonight," he said.

I stared at Jimmy for a moment, not able to gather a response. "I can't believe that, Jimmy," I finally said.

"Believe it. It's the truth," he insisted. And with that, he released his grip on my arm. I said nothing and slowly made my exit from his car.

I was stunned. As I walked to my car, Jimmy's words echoed through my mind. *Your father didn't help you in there tonight.* In the darkness of the Brooklyn night, the words began to sink in, and I began to analyze my father's actions and Jimmy's conclusion. I thought about my father's situation and how he would have handled it. I imagined he had probably taken the high road. He didn't throw me under the bus, but he didn't throw me a life-raft either. He must have played dumb. I could almost hear the words coming from his mouth. *"I'm on parole. My son handles all the business. I don't know what he did or didn't do. You will have to ask him."*

It had been the right move for him in that situation. In fact, I had set it up that way to protect him from a parole violation. Even so, it hurt to realize that he could have taken a stronger stand on my behalf without jeopardizing himself. My dad was a respected caporegime, a former underboss. He could have told my accusers that the rumors were all nonsense, and I would never do anything to dishonor the family or deceive my superiors. He could have put the situation to rest before I even entered the room. But he didn't, and his silence had kept me in harm's way.

Dad must've known the position he would take before he went into the meeting. He knew he would be okay. But could he have been so sure it would turn out that way for me? What if I hadn't been able to "somehow talk my way out of it," as Jimmy said? Would I be lying in the trunk of someone's car right now instead of driving home in my own?

My father probably went to sleep that night feeling proud. He had obeyed an order. He had walked into that room without fear, his head held high. He had emerged unscathed from the accusations that were whirling around the Franzese crew, and he had maintained his honorable status as one of the family's most respected elder statesmen. I wished I could view it the same way. Instead, I felt like a fool, like I was the ultimate sucker for walking into that room believing that I might not come out of it alive. I had placed my life in my father's hands, and he had let me down.

The drive home that night was one of the most introspective experiences of my life. My father had been my idol. I loved him dearly, and I knew he loved me. I could not envision having a closer bond with any other man. *How could he have let the mob life separate us?* I thought. *Can I ever fully trust him again?* The events of that night spun my thoughts far beyond my relationship with my father: *If I can't place my trust in Dad, is there anyone I can ever really trust?*

I realized it was a mistake to have placed so much faith in my father, even if he didn't intentionally say or do anything to hurt me in that meeting. The position he took that night was a result of the "mob mentality" he had developed over the course of a lifetime on the streets of Brooklyn. In a way, it was an act of instinctual self-preservation on his part. For maybe the first time in my life, Dad was not someone to be idolized, either as a "made man" or as my father, and I certainly was not his doting little boy any longer. The stakes were much higher for me now than they were the day my stepbrother was ousted from the house to hop around on the freshly fallen snow. Clearly my father would not always come through for me, and he would in fact let me down at times, intentionally or not. I saw that placing all my trust in Dad was an unfair burden for him. In fact, placing all my trust in anyone was an unfair burden for any human being, myself included. *How many times in the past had I let someone down?* I wondered.

In an obscure home on a quiet street in Brooklyn, on a night when I came eerily close to losing my life, I learned a lesson that would serve me well as both a made man in La Cosa Nostra and later as a husband, father and friend. As I drove home that night, I vowed to never again place my complete trust in any man.

The feds in Brooklyn finally broke their losing streak against the Colombo family this week when they nailed two Colombo hoods for the execution murder of former consigliere Vincent (Jimmy) Angellino. DeLucia drove Angellino to his execution and Legrano helped wrap his body for disposal, according to testimony by key prosecution witnesses Carmine Sessa and Rocco Cagno. Sessa, who later took Angellino's spot as consigliere, was the trigger man; Angellino was killed in Cagno's Kenilworth, N.J. home.
—New York Daily News, 8/16/1995

CHAPTER 5:
THE TRIALS

For troubles without number
surround me; my sins have
overtaken me, and I cannot see.

—Psalm 40:12

THE TRIAL CAME to a close in the first week of May 1985. After five full days of deliberations, the jury finally reached a verdict. After the twelve jurors took their place in the jury box, the Honorable Judge Leonard Sand ordered all defendants to rise and face the jury. Let the heart pounding begin! There were twenty-nine counts of criminal behavior in the indictment; I was charged in seven of them. A conviction on any one of the counts would land me in prison for a long time. If I went down on all seven, the Feds would surely throw away the key.

It took an hour and a half for the jury to read the verdict on all twenty-nine counts, one at a time against each defendant individually, as they were required to do by law. Seven times I heard the word "Not" before the word "Guilty" as the jury foreman called out my name. Of the fifteen defendants on trial, seven were acquitted. The remaining eight were less fortunate. I had pulled off yet another victory against the very formidable Department of Justice.

But I wasn't about to bask in the glory of a bittersweet victory. The years of investigations, subpoenas, grand jury appearances, undercover informants, search warrants, arrests, and jury trials were starting to take their toll. And it wasn't over yet. The government wasn't about to put its powerful tail between its legs, slink away, and concede victory, not to a Mafia prince. I was the hunted, the government was the hunter, and the hunter was about to aim at me again.

On December 16, 1985, just three days before Gambino family boss Paul Castellano was gunned down on orders from

John Gotti, the late "Dapper Don" himself, the Long Island task force threw down its hammer. Members of my crew and I were slammed with yet another massive racketeering indictment, this time from the Feds in the Eastern District of New York. Some of the charges, including loan sharking and extortion, were similar to those I had beaten in the Southern District case. There were a few additional charges that were unique to my own personal infamous misdeeds: wire fraud, labor racketeering, and the one charge for which I had the most exposure, tax fraud.

The Feds claimed that the wholesale gasoline business I had presided over was, in fact, a massive scheme to defraud Uncle Sam out of a few billion dollars in gasoline tax money, and that I was mastermind of the operation. The G-Men actually had it right this time. At the height of our operation, my gasoline tax-fraud enterprise was moving about a half-billion gallons of fuel per month—do the math. The government and media tend to exaggerate their claims at times, but the money flowing into my operation was, to say the least, substantial.

Just a few months earlier, on a quiet street in Brooklyn, I had squared off against the brass of the Colombo family to answer charges concerning my business. The stakes were high for me then—my life! And now, I was summoned to Brooklyn once again to answer charges concerning my business, this time in a federal court-house. Once again, the stakes would be high—my freedom!

CHAPTER 6:
THE BEAUTY

You have stolen my heart with
one glance of your eyes.

—Song of Solomon 4:9

MICHAEL FRANZESE, the guy who NBC's Tom Brokaw once described as a "prince of the Mafia, as rich as royalty," was about to send a shockwave through the hallowed offices of McDonald's strike force that would echo all the way through the mobbed-up social clubs of Brooklyn. Dad's lofty plans for me to take control of the Colombo family were about to be broadsided, and from the most unlikely of sources. No one would have predicted that in 1985, after a string of legal victories that would rival the record of John Gotti himself, I was about to fold up the family tent, throw in the towel, and admit defeat at the hands of the government's mob-busters. My decision to plead guilty to the pending indictment took everyone by surprise, including my lawyer, John Jacobs. "You could beat this rap," I remember him saying. Jacobs was a fighter, all right. For a cool half-a-million-dollar trial fee, what lawyer wouldn't be? All a lawyer has to lose is the case—not his freedom, his family, and certainly not his money.

But I knew something Jacobs didn't know. The government had a secret weapon that came straight from the streets. No one else was aware of it at the time, not even the G-Men themselves. And although this weapon would benefit the prosecution, it would also one day change my life forever and most certainly for the better. It wasn't a co-defendant-turned-snitch or some blockbuster revelation caught on tape. It didn't come from the streets of Brooklyn, Queens, or Long Island. This bombshell came from the streets of Anaheim, California, from Disneyland's own backyard. This secret and powerful weapon was a gorgeous, twenty-year-old Mexican beauty.

I met Camille Garcia just months before the Giuliani trial began, while I was producing a dance movie in south Florida. I first saw her lifting herself from the pool at the Marina Bay Club, a trendy hotel in the heart of Fort Lauderdale. Like a gorgeous figure in a Pepsi commercial, she appeared to move in slow motion as she ascended the ladder and shook the glimmering droplets of water from her long, coffee-colored hair. Her face glistened in the blazing sunlight that accentuated her big brown eyes and pouty lips. Her firm dancer's body appeared to be exploding out of her bikini, yet there was an innocence about her movements that suggested she was clueless as to how breathtaking she really was. She was, without a doubt, the most beautiful, exotic woman I had ever seen. I was completely mesmerized, unable to take my eyes off of her. I had been with more than my share of women, but never before had the mere sight of a woman had such an effect on me. With all that was swirling around me at the time, it was rare that my thoughts weren't consumed with the continuing drama that was my life. But as I stared at this young dancer by the pool, all the hassles of my business, the mob, and the government's relentless pursuit of me vanished from my mind.

For the remainder of the day, I tried to keep my mind on business, but the image of Camille, "Cammy" to her friends, kept intruding. I remembered an Italian old wives' tale about men being "hit by a thunderbolt" because of the effect a particular woman had on them. According to the tale, there didn't seem to be any explanation; it just happened. I had laughed about the idea in the past, but now I wasn't so sure. My own personal "thunderbolt" certainly seemed to have appeared out of nowhere.

But I had too much going on in my life to even think about falling for a woman. Mob life is not conducive to a satisfying marriage. That's one part the TV series "The Sopranos" got right. My commitment to the life had made me adopt a personal policy not to engage in any activity that would distract me from my business. Even drugs and alcohol were kept strictly off-limits. A voice in the back of my mind urged me to do the same with this young woman.

The close, family-like atmosphere of a movie crew on location made my plan to avoid Cammy Garcia almost impossible. I kept bumping into her in the hotel lobby or on the movie set, and every time I caught a glimpse of her, it stopped me dead in my tracks. Each new sighting burned another image into my mind. The mere sight of this woman was enough to drive me crazy. Any chance I had to avoid getting involved was obliterated one afternoon when I was invited to watch the dancers rehearse. Seeing her gorgeous body move through the rhythmic beats of Shannon's "Let the Music Play" did me in. I could no longer resist my desire for her. I decided to go for it.

For the next week, every time I bumped into her, I made her promise to drop by my suite for a visit. At least five times she agreed to meet me, and at least five times she failed to show. But the little cat-and-mouse game she was unconsciously playing made me even more determined to pursue her. I suspected Cammy was unsure how to respond to me. She didn't want to be rude, but neither did she want to get involved with someone she perceived to be an older, sophisticated businessman and movie producer.

Over the next few weeks, I divided my time between the streets of New York and the movie set, flying back and forth almost every other day. When away from the set, I couldn't wait to get back to continue my pursuit of Cammy. She still kept her distance, moving away from me as gracefully as she moved to the beats on the dance floor.

Finally, one evening, my persistence paid off. I was invited to join a group of dancers and crew members at Shooters, a popular Fort Lauderdale night spot. A few of my own "crew" members were planning to be there, and I decided to go. When I arrived, Cammy was sitting among the dancers, talking to one of my guys. I immediately displaced him from his seat and, for the first time since seeing her by the pool, I was able to engage her in a meaningful conversation.

We talked for the next couple of hours, and it was as if we were the only ones there. We chatted about the movie, her dancing, and the rest of her life. I wanted to know everything about her.

Cammy told me about growing up in the working class neighborhood of Norwalk, southeast of Los Angeles, and of her family's eventual move to Disney's neighborhood in the city of Anaheim. She talked glowingly about her mother Irma, who was a deep woman of faith, and about her six brothers and sisters. Cammy told how her father, Seferino, was a radical Chicano-rights activist who had been arrested eight times during the turbulent 1970s. Some of those arrests included violent confrontations with the

Norwalk police. He had been roughed up pretty badly at times. *Maybe she won't be so taken aback when she learns of my involvement in the mob,* I thought to myself.

We talked for hours, remaining at the table long after everyone had left. From that time on, we were inseparable—spending hours together, talking about anything and everything. I had never known anyone like her. She was gorgeous, yet innocent, and she carried herself with class and integrity that was uncommon for a woman her age. But even then, I had no idea what an impact this young dancer was about to have on my life.

Ultimately, Cammy became a star witness, whose blockbuster testimony would dramatically alter the course of my life, but not in a way that anyone could have imagined, myself included. She wouldn't give her testimony under oath. No jury would have to evaluate her honesty. No defense lawyer would get to cross-examine her. In fact, she would never take the witness stand. Her testimony could not be impeached.

She witnessed to me on the beaches of south Florida, while driving on the freeways of Los Angeles, and while dining on a Ruth Chris steak or a bowl of fettuccine alfredo. Cammy was a Christian—a young woman of faith who talked about her relationship with Jesus Christ, how she had surrendered her life to Him several years earlier, and why she truly believed I needed to do the same. Here I was, the mob's "Long Island Don" as I came to be known, getting a dose of religion from this young Latin beauty.

Truth be told, I quickly fell very much in love with Cammy and became determined to have her in my life. However, the only *relationship* that interested me was the one I wanted with her, and the only *surrender* I would consider was to the Feds, so I could ultimately have that life with her. And as far as I was concerned, although I politely listened to her talk about Jesus, He wasn't getting anything else from me.

But hearing her talk of God as she did made me realize that, in order to be with her, I would have to make some drastic changes in my life. The lifestyle in which I was embroiled was a direct contradiction to everything she believed in and wanted for us. A future with Cammy would first require my getting off the government's radar screen. A guilty plea, some time in prison and a permanent move to the Golden State would send a message to the G-men that The Long Island Don was hanging up his six-shooter and calling it quits. Then, I thought, all I had to do was keep my nose clean.

It would not be easy. The thought of being separated from Cammy by prison bars for any length of time was excruciatingly painful. She told me she would trust in God to work it all out. I never saw someone pray so much. But the way I looked at it, I needed all the help I could get, because the Feds were only part of the challenge I would face. Being with Cammy meant turning away from the organization I gave my life to that Halloween night so many years ago. It meant breaking the bond I shared with the made men of the family, my crew. It meant renouncing my blood oath—the vow I made to honor and respect La Cosa Nostra. Nobody does that, not without joining up with the Feds and entering a Witness Protection Program. For me, that wasn't an option. I didn't have it in for my former associates; I wasn't seeking revenge on the mob or on those who lived the life with me. I just wanted out.

But by far, the most difficult part of my decision was that it meant breaking ties with my legendary father. He would *never* accept my decision to walk away, not Dad. He was as much a part of the mob as the mob was a part of him. He was a mobster in life; surely he would be a mobster in death, and he would expect me to be the same. We were both married to the mob, and the vow we took upon tying that knot was crystal clear: "Until death do us part!"

CHAPTER 7:
THE PLAN

"For my thoughts are not your thoughts, neither are your ways my ways," declares the LORD.

—Isaiah 55:8

DESPITE THE MANY CHALLENGES I would inevitably face, I was intent on changing the course of my life and marrying Cammy. So, fresh off a victory in the Giuliani trial, I wasted no time doing just that. The day after the verdict was announced, Cammy and I bolted from New York and quietly tied the knot in a Christian chapel on the famed Las Vegas strip. Although I was raised a Catholic, I had no problem with taking vows in a Christian chapel for Cammy's sake. She was serious about her commitment to Jesus, while my commitment to Him was chilly at best. In fact, my interest in Jesus only existed because I kept hearing about Him from her. I would have listened to anything she wanted to discuss if it meant I could get to know her better. I must admit, though, all her talk about God did provide me with some food for thought. I was taught about the concept of accepting Christ, the gift of grace, and the forgiveness of sins in Catholic school, but the message packed more of a punch coming from a beautiful woman with whom I was madly in love.

As it turned out, the quiet Vegas service was just a warm-up for what was to follow. Cammy deserved a celebration, and I was determined to give her one she would never forget. Much like Italian families, Mexican families tend to be quite large, and Cammy's was no exception. My dad was one of nineteen children; her dad was one of twenty-three. Apparently, neither of our grandparents believed in birth control! They were also fun-loving folks who really enjoyed a party, so I decided to give them one.

On July 27, 1985, Cammy and I took our vows once again, this time in a Christian church in Westwood, California, just a stone's throw away from the UCLA campus. We celebrated our joyous occasion along with five hundred of our closest friends and Cammy's family at an elaborate reception at the Beverly Hilton Hotel. It was a night to remember. Her family had a wedding tradition called the "dollar dance" in which guests pay a dollar or more to dance with the bride or the groom. I thought it would never end. I could have laid down a nice bet with our earnings.

As we celebrated into the night, thoughts of my impending showdown with the government, the family, and my father kept invading my mind. The odds against my overcoming all three to have a life with Cammy had to be at least a hundred to one. As I stared at my beautiful new bride, I wondered just how long we would have to enjoy our newly taken vows. The bookies would have set the over/under at five years. The smart money would have taken the under.

Throughout the early months of our marriage, Cammy continued to encourage me to have a relationship with Christ, and she assured me that if I were to place my faith in Him, He would guide me through the difficult times that lay ahead. But Cammy could have no idea just how difficult those times would be. I never really opened up to her about the challenges I faced. I wanted to protect her from them as long as I could. Besides, could I honestly tell her that quitting the mob might leave me a dead man?

In desperate realization that I was going to need help from *somewhere* to pull this off, I began to listen more intently to what she had to say. Cammy's encouragement finally had such an influence on me that, in a meeting I had with Dr. Myron Taylor, the pastor who married us, I actually said a prayer and accepted Christ as my personal Savior. The kindly, white-haired minister spoke to me in a way that made me want to open up to him about my secret life. I never felt the need to do that with anyone before. But this man spoke so confidently about Jesus and how He knew my heart and would forgive my sins if I truly confessed, no matter how grievous those sins were. "Sin is sin," I remember him telling me. "The ground at the foot of the cross is level." He said if I would lay my sins there, they would be washed away by the blood of Jesus, and He would secure my place in heaven for all of eternity.

What Dr. Taylor had to say sounded good to me. In the mob life, I lived every day in violation of the laws of God and man. I was a sinner, plain and simple. Why wouldn't I want to be forgiven? If a simple prayer of acceptance was all it took, I was ready. At that moment, I wanted forgiveness for my sins, but nothing more. Cammy's idea of surrendering to Jesus and giving Him control of my life would not be part of my program. I would need to be pro-active in dealing with the government and my mob family; I could not expect to sit back and let Jesus handle them for me. Most Italians grow up under the belief that God helps those who help themselves. I was no different. And besides, I had a plan.

Three months after I was charged in the Eastern District indictment, I entered into an all-inclusive plea agreement with the government. The deal carried with it a ten-year prison term, followed by five years of probation and fifteen million dollars in fines and restitution for my misdeeds. Since I was indicted under the old federal law, I would be eligible for parole in forty-two months. If I kept my nose clean, I would be home with Cammy in less then four years. As part of the arrangement, I would do my time in Terminal Island, a federal prison just forty minutes from our home in Los Angeles. Cammy would be able to visit often, and I would do all I could to make her comfortable while we were apart. Although the separation would be difficult, she understood that it was necessary if we were to have a meaningful life together. And, as always, she believed that God would see us through.

Once the matter with the Feds was resolved, I turned my attention to the second part of my plan—quitting the mob. Convicted mobsters from the East Coast are not normally assigned to a federal prison in southern California. While in prison, my contact with the guys from New York would be limited. Mobsters on parole and probation are forbidden by policy to associate with convicted felons or other mob guys. I was hoping that being on parole and probation would allow me to quietly disassociate myself from my crew. After ten years, the family would forget about me, and Cammy and I would live happily ever after in the Golden State. That was my plan—but it didn't quite work out that way.

About a year into my imprisonment, a reporter from *Life* magazine decided to do a story on me—whom they dubbed the "Yuppie Don"—and my future in the mob. My mob activities had been highly publicized over the years, and the publicity certainly added to the government's vendetta against both me and my dad. That vendetta was sure to be resumed upon my release from prison. Part of my overall plan was to maintain a low profile, so I would drop off of the G-Men's radar screen. The last thing I needed was another major story to push me right back into the limelight. The reporter was very persistent in his requests to the warden to interview me for the story. In one of my more boneheaded moves, I agreed to the interview, believing the story might be less toxic if I were to provide some commentary. Wrong!

Within a few weeks of granting the interview, the warden summoned me to his office and asked if I had a death wish. Then he showed me the hot-off-the-press *Life* magazine article. There it was, in a four-page, full-color spread complete with pictures, a headline that screamed, "Quitting the Mafia," and a story that began with the following paragraphs:

> There's an old saying that the only way to leave the Mafia is in a coffin. Members are pledged to secrecy, and to quit would be to

arouse suspicion that you are cooperating with the police or federal agents. Such breaches of faith are punished with death. Michael Franzese says he is willing to take that risk. He will not betray his former crime associates and then disappear into the federal Witness Protection Program... If he holds to what he has promised... It will mark the first time that a high-ranking member of the Mafia will walk away from his past.

My heart sank. The reporter had placed his own spin on my efforts to let the government think I was going straight. Although the G-Men might have gotten my message, to say the article did not sit well with the guys back East would be an understatement. The Feds had already told the warden that the reaction on the street was not conducive to my health. It was all I could do to convince him not to place me in solitary for my own protection. And to make matters worse, the Feds viewed the article as a signal that I would be willing to cooperate in investigations against my mob associates. In a nutshell, my efforts to exercise damage control by granting the reporter an interview totally backfired. In one gigantic blunder, I managed to alienate the mob, place my life in danger, and rekindle the government's interest in me, even if this time it was for a different purpose.

I could never have imagined the course of events that would follow that *Life* magazine article, events that would have nearly everyone in law enforcement who knew my story predicting that I would soon be a victim of a classic mob hit. During the next four years of my confinement, as the saying goes, all hell broke loose. I had death threats, periods of solitary confinement, and pressure from the government to cooperate against the family. The Feds offered to place me in the Witness Protection Program and give me a new identity, so that Cammy and I would be able to start fresh when all the testifying was over. We had two little daughters—the first conceived before I went to prison, the second during some time spent in a halfway house just prior to my incarceration. Living in hiding wasn't the change I was seeking for myself or my family. But how else would I pull it off? How would I go from being a Colombo family man to a family man, husband, and father to my children? And would La Cosa Nostra allow me to live long enough to enjoy such a blessing? Honestly, I didn't have a clue.

Throughout my imprisonment, Cammy continued to encourage me in my faith, and she leaned heavily on hers to get her through what was a very difficult time for us both. Although I had been baptized within months of my release from prison and fully intended to try to live the Christian life, I was simply unable to do it. The idea of having God in control of my life, and of me not being in control, was so foreign to my thinking that I couldn't receive it. I was so used to doing everything for myself that I now thought I had to somehow get through my probation period and escape the mob's wrath by using my own wits. Accepting Christ as my Lord and Savior was not a guarantee I would be spared from the mob's vengeance; I understood that. It was not part of the contract God made with me. Now that my place in eternity had been secured, He could have allowed my life to end mob-style, with a bullet to the back of the head. God could have allowed for mob justice to take its course on earth while He prepared for me a place in heaven.

The months I spent on probation were among the most challenging of my life, even more difficult than the time I spent in prison. I was overwhelmed by the weight of the adversity I faced in almost every area. Between the G-men's relentless attempts to have me testify against the mob and the mob's attempts to have me eliminated, I rarely had a moment's peace. The cost of my legal defense and that of supporting Cammy and the kids during my years of incarceration had drained me of millions. I needed to earn a living—not an easy task for a federally supervised former mobster with a price on his head, especially in the free-wheeling city of Los Angeles. I was living and working outside of my element. With the men in the wing-tipped shoes *and* those with the pin-striped suits hot on my tail, I just could not get anything going in the area of business. I felt like a fish out of water, hunted by a school of mobster-eating sharks. And after thirteen months of evading my predators, I was about to get eaten.

CHAPTER 8:
THE SURRENDER

*Trust in the LORD with all
your heart and lean not on your
own understanding; in all your ways
acknowledge him, and he will
make your paths straight.*

–Proverbs 3:5-6

ON THE MORNING OF November 13, 1991, while making a routine visit to the local bank, my world came crashing down around me. As I exited the bank, I was abducted by a team of federal and state law enforcement agents. Before I could say "fuggedaboutit,"

I was arrested, shoved into a paddy-wagon, and headed back to the slammer. There's a saying that goes something like this, "You can take the boy out of Brooklyn, but you can't take Brooklyn out of the boy." I had engaged in some questionable financial transactions, and it gave the Feds all the ammunition they needed to charge me with violating the conditions of my probation. Old habits die hard, especially when they were developed in the mobbed-up streets of Brooklyn. Turning to Christ might have cleansed me of my sins, but a full surrender of my heart and mind would be a process. And for me, that process was about to shift into high gear.

On the drive down to the lock-up, the agents made it very clear that the wrath of the Justice Department had come down on me, and that I should plan on spending a very long time in the Big House. I was charged with prior crimes that they had only recently heard about, courtesy of the newest wave of informants seeking a sweet-heart deal for themselves. Apparently, my reluctance to testify against my former mob associates did not sit well with the Feds in Brooklyn, and when the G-men get mad, they tend to get even. I was taken to the federal jail in downtown Los Angeles, where I was booked and placed in administrative detention—"the Hole."

When the steel door of my cell slammed closed, it was as if a huge boulder had crashed in front of my entire future. I can't begin to adequately describe what I was feeling in the first moments when I was left completely alone. I was hurting worse then I had ever hurt before. Part of what I was feeling, of course, was the dread of spending more years behind bars without Cammy and the children. But it was worse then that. This time, the money had all but run out, and what was left in the bank the government would surely confiscate. *How would she and our children survive? How would she endure yet another round of lonely nights following heart-wrenching days alongside me in the prison visiting room?* She had endured so much heartache during the past seven years; would her faith in God carry her through what was certain to be the greatest challenge to our marriage yet? Or would the strain of it all be too much for her to bear? The thought of losing her along with my children was tearing me up inside.

Adding to my anguish and worry for the welfare of Cammy and the kids was the thought of a soon-to-be-published book about my life. The book was supposed to be a wonderful way of showing what "God had done" in my life. It portrayed a man who had been about as lost as any one man could be, but who had been changed by accepting Jesus Christ as His Lord and Savior. Cammy had encouraged me over and over to surrender control of my life to Jesus. I refused, believing I could handle my own affairs. And there I was, in an orange jumpsuit sitting in a cell buried deep within the cinder-block walls of the federal jail. *What a great example of God's work in my life*, I thought. I was an embarrassment to myself, to my family, and to my God, and I had no one to blame but myself.

On top of all of this was the realization that I could spend the rest of my life in the Hole, a prison within the prison. The Feds would never risk placing me in the general population, not with a mob contract on my head.

As I lay on the cot in that cell, I was drowning in a feeling of total devastation, completely overwhelmed by what I perceived to be the hopelessness of my predicament. Hopelessness is by far the most painful of all emotions, and it was one I had never experienced. For mob guys, life is all about controlling people and situations. But at that moment, I was totally helpless and out of answers, like holding a gun with an empty chamber. I felt as if the world I had come to know had been irreparably destroyed, taken down by the weight of the Mafia chain I had so meticulously linked around my neck. The pain I felt in my heart was excruciating. In my thoughts, I cried out to God to relieve me of the pain, to take me that night, because I honestly could not bear to go on. I wanted out.

As I lay there with my head buried under the weight of my folded arms, a prison guard walked by my cell on a routine bed-check. "You okay, Franzese?" I heard him say. "You don't look so good."

What would you expect from a dead man? I wanted to say. "I don't feel so good tonight," I muttered.

With that he disappeared, only to return a short time later. "This might help you out," he whispered. I heard a thump. Through glassy eyes, I noticed that a book had landed on the floor of my cell. As my eyes gradually cleared, I saw that it was a Bible. The guard had pushed a Bible through the slot in the door. *Is he kidding me?* I thought. A bottle of Valium would have served me far better.

God was not what I wanted at that moment. In fact, I was angry with God. *Is this the reward I get for accepting His Son? The loss of my family and a lifetime in prison? Did Cammy lead me to Christ only to lose me to the Department of Justice?* As I stared down at the Bible, my emotions began to boil over. Within moments, I bolted off the cot, picked up the Bible, and hurled it against the wall. It dropped to the floor and I glared at it further, wanting to somehow transfer the anger I felt to the Author of that book. As my flood of emotion began to subside, I realized it was only me and God in that cell, and the last thing I needed was another enemy. I bent down and picked up the Bible.

I began to leaf through it, wanting to see something, *anything* that would give me some hope that I was not abandoned. I came upon the Old Testament book of Proverbs, and a verse in Chapter 16 immediately caught my attention: "When a man's ways are pleasing to the Lord, even his enemies are at peace with him."

The verse struck me. I had nothing but enemies that night. *Was there a message in that verse for me? Was God responding to me?* I looked up to see my reflection in the scratched and broken plastic mirror affixed to the wall above the stainless-steel toilet. I asked myself, *Have your ways been at all pleasing to the Lord? Have you really tried to live a godly life?* Sure, I believed in Jesus, accepted Him as God's only Son. I had that much in common with the devil. Cammy told me I would need to *surrender* my life to Jesus. And, like the devil, I had been unwilling to do that.

But now, those words began to comfort me. *Was God trying to tell me something?* As I continued to scan through Proverbs, I came to yet another verse that stopped me dead-cold. Proverbs Chapter 3, verses 5 and 6 read, "Trust in the Lord with all your heart and lean not on your own understanding; in all your ways acknowledge Him and He will make your paths straight."

The words began to reverberate through my brain. *Trust in the Lord. Acknowledge Him in all I do. Make my paths straight.* I had heard those words before. Throughout all of my struggles, Cammy told me I needed to trust in Jesus to pull me through. Cammy's mother, Irma, was the most godly woman I had ever met, and she had told me to leave all of my burdens at the foot of the cross. Dr. Taylor had told me to do the same, encouraging me to be like the apostle Paul and surrender myself completely to Jesus; then He could work through me to fulfill God's purpose in my life. They all said I needed to surrender my heart totally and completely to Jesus and trust in Him to see me through the tough times. They said I couldn't do it by myself. But I refused to listen. I believed that God helped those who helped themselves. That was the way of the street, the way a "real man" would handle his struggles. And besides, seventeen years in the mob had taught me that placing trust in another could end up costing a man his life. I had vowed never to place my complete trust in anyone, and I learned it the hard way in that obscure home on a quiet street in Brooklyn.

But that was before today, the darkest day of my existence on this earth, before the feeling of total hopelessness had left me desperate and broken, faced with the prospect of losing everything and everyone I held dear to me. Just moments before the stroke of midnight Pacific Standard Time on November 13, 1991, with nowhere to go and no one else to turn to, I dropped to my knees and promised God that if He would come to my aid, I would *offer* my life to Jesus. I begged Him to ease the excruciating pain that had overtaken me. But I also challenged Him to prove that I could trust in His Son not only for my salvation, but for His promise to comfort me in a time of dire need.

A voice inside of me was telling me to read on, and I listened. Over the next few hours, I poured through the gospels of Mark and John and the letters of Paul. As I continued to read about the life of Jesus, the pain in my heart began to subside. The feeling of hopelessness that had held my mind and heart like a vice began to loosen its death-grip. When I read in 2 Corinthians 12:9 how Jesus had comforted Paul in a time of his suffering by telling him, "My grace is sufficient for you, for my power is made perfect in weakness," I felt like Jesus was talking to me. He was assuring me that He was going to work this all out, that He would be there throughout this ordeal and would never leave my side. Why else would I have been directed to that verse during my moment of weakness? Some might believe it to be a coincidence. I say God's timing is perfect.

From that moment on, my life would never be the same. In the years to follow, I found my true hero, both in this life and in the next. Jesus showed me first-hand His power to comfort an aching heart that was sinking into the depths of distress. On that night and throughout my entire second term of imprisonment, I honestly felt that I was not alone, that Jesus was in that cell with me. And in return, I promised my Savior that I would trust Him with my life.

CHAPTER 9:
THE CHALLENGE

Test everything.
Hold on to the good.

—1 Thessalonians 5:21

THE "VERY LONG TIME" the Feds promised I would spend incarcerated amounted to an additional four-year sentence, imposed on me by the Honorable Eugene H. Nickerson. With time off for good behavior, I would spend the next thirty-five months and twenty-three days in the federal lock-up, twenty-nine of those months in total isolation. The Bureau of Prisons was not about to place me in the general population, where any mob "wannabe" looking to gain favor with the boys in Brooklyn could try to collect on the contract placed on my head.

Total isolation is certainly not pleasant. I would have preferred to be housed among the general population, where I could take advantage of some of the "amenities" afforded normal federal inmates. I would have gladly taken my chances on the yard in exchange for a daily shower, an occasional ray of sunlight, and a breath of fresh air. But now, looking back, I realize that amidst all of the madness that engulfed my life during that time, God was at work. Because of Cammy's faithful prayers, He had laid claim to my soul.

But even though God held a place in my heart, He still did not have ownership of it, and He had not yet captured my mind, either. I believed Jesus would take care of my spirit in heaven, but it was still up to me to handle my human affairs on earth. Like most mob guys, membership in La Cosa Nostra had made me quite cynical—a made man had to be if he was to survive the street life. No one was going to sell me a bridge in Brooklyn. If the evidence was not there, I wasn't buying it.

So despite my battered emotional state that first evening, I found myself struggling to surrender my life completely without assurances that this time, my faith would not be misplaced. As much as I loved my wife, neither she nor anyone else was going to make me commit my life to someone or something that may not have my best interests at heart. For me to *surrender* my human life to Jesus, as I once surrendered to La Cosa Nostra, Jesus would have to appeal to my intellect. I had to believe beyond any doubt that He would have my back, regardless of the circumstances I faced. Only then would I be able to trust Him to guide me through the turbulent waters that lay ahead.

I can vividly recall reading through the pages of my prison Bible that first night and challenging God, boldly calling on the Creator of the universe to *prove* to me that what Cammy, Irma, and Dr. Taylor had been telling me was true: that the Bible is truly *His* word, and that Jesus is truly *His* Son and the Savior of all those who put their trust in Him. I wasn't about to place "blind" faith in my heavenly Father as I once did in my earthly father. I wanted proof that if I trusted His Son with my life I would not be abandoned, as I had been on that obscure street in Brooklyn just a few years earlier. There would be no *surrender* to the Son of

God as there had been to a secret oath that now left me fighting for my life.

But on that darkest of nights, God was more then willing to accept my challenge. I now believe He knew that, in order to claim ownership of my heart, soul, *and* will, He would need my complete and undivided attention. He would need to eliminate all the distractions of the outside world. And He would need to bring me to my knees and strip me of my reliance on my own prowess to deliver myself from a fate from which He alone could provide an escape. An isolated prison cell would afford God the opportunity to continue the process He started years ago when that beautiful young woman emerged from those sparkling blue waters of that exotic swimming pool. But make no mistake, His plan and purpose for my life could only be revealed when I surrendered *completely* to His Son, for it is only *in* Jesus and *through* Jesus that God implements His plans for our lives.

I have heard people criticize Christianity on more than one occasion, saying it demands a blind faith that the Bible is truly the Word of God and that Jesus Christ is the risen Savior of all mankind. In fact, several years ago I read a pretty harsh article written by HBO's Bill Maher in which he declared Christians are forbidden to question any information contained in the Bible—that we must be like robots, following the written word like lambs being led to their inevitable slaughter.

I hereby challenge Mr. Maher and anyone else to direct me to any chapter or verse in the Bible that demands its readers have blind faith in any portion of God's word. Nothing could be further from the truth. If God had wanted a world of robots, human beings would not have "free will." Actually, we can choose to believe anything we want, including God's word as it is contained in the Bible.

As I said before, my decision to surrender my life to Jesus wasn't going to be a blind one. (One critical decision made out of blind faith is enough in anyone's lifetime.) I made my decision to become a follower of Jesus as a result of the reliable, credible evidence I discovered after a sincere and honest search for the truth. This evidence established beyond a reasonable doubt (which is the standard of proof required to convict a defendant in a criminal proceeding in the United States) that the Bible is truly the word of God and that Jesus is truly the risen Savior of all mankind. Twenty-five years of experience in the criminal justice system—including five criminal trials of my own and three of my father's, a multitude of grand jury appearances, several parole hearings and appellate court proceedings, and seven years in prison—clearly qualified me to competently analyze evidence. Trust me, I can measure up to any criminal defense attorney in that regard. And at the end of the day, it was the honest evaluation of the facts in support of Christian beliefs that brought me to surrender my life to Jesus, not some miraculous incarnation or a voice from heaven. I wasn't in need of a "crutch" when I searched for the truth; I was in need of a *Savior*. And I believe with all my heart and soul that I found one in the overwhelming evidence that was processed in my brain, cultivated in my heart, and solidified through my experiences.

CHAPTER 10:
THE EVIDENCE

*...I myself have carefully
investigated everything from the
beginning ... so that you may know
the certainty of the things you
have been taught.*

—Luke 1:3-4

I SPENT NEARLY every day of my twenty-nine months in the Hole pouring through the Bible, reading chapters and verses over and over again, intent on either proving its reliability or dismissing it as the ill-conceived ramblings of a group of ancient religious fanatics. For the first time in my life, I would give the Bible a thorough and honest reading, applying my sense of reason and my life experiences in evaluating what was recorded on its pages. I would give God the opportunity to make a believer out of me, and it wasn't going to be an easy sell.

The objective data for the truth of Christianity comes from two primary sources: the Bible, and the legal historical evidence. So I began my search for the truth with the Old Testament Book of Proverbs. I was particularly amazed at the wisdom of King Solomon of ancient Israel, whose writings comprise the greater part of that book. I compared his teachings to those of Nicolo dei Bernardo Machiavelli, the sixteenth century Italian philosopher and diplomat. The Machiavellian philosophy, which is best explained in his political treatise *The Prince,* is the cornerstone upon which La Cosa Nostra was built. *The Prince* is to the mob what the Bible is to Christians. Where Solomon's mission statement and purpose in his writings was "... for attaining wisdom and discipline, for understanding words of insight; for acquiring a disciplined and prudent life, doing what is right and just and fair," Machiavelli believed that any evil action can be justified if it is done for a good purpose. He said, "…in the actions of all men… one judges by the result." His philosophy was, simply stated, the end justifies the means.

Comparing the philosophies of these two men really caused me to reflect on my life. As a made man, I had ascribed to the Machiavellian philosophy as a way of life. I justified living almost every day in violation of the laws of man and consciously avoided accountability to an almighty God. In reading Proverbs, I realized how flawed this Machiavellian way of living really was. I asked myself, *Since defecting from the life, have I honestly been doing that much better? Am I really trying to live the kind of moral life that Solomon professed?* "All a man's ways seem right to him, but the Lord weighs the heart," (Proverbs 21:2). I wondered how God was weighing my heart.

In continuing to read Proverbs, it was as if each verse was intended for me, yet it was written thousands of years ago. Reading the book was like looking into the window of my soul. I remember asking myself, *Can any man really be so wise, so profound in his teachings, or was He truly inspired by God as Christians believe?* I got my answer later on while reading the Old Testament Book of

1 Kings, in which God rewarded Solomon for loving Him as his father, King David, did before him. "...Ask for whatever you want me to give you," said the Lord (3:5). And Solomon responded, "So give your servant a discerning heart to govern your people and to distinguish between right and wrong..." (3:9). And the Lord responded, "Since you have asked for this and not for long life or wealth for yourself, nor have you asked for the death of your enemies but for discernment in administering justice, I will do what you have asked. I will give you a wise and discerning heart, so that there will never have been anyone like you, nor will there ever be" (3:11-12). God Himself provided the evidence to support what my common sense revealed to me about King Solomon. By God's own decree, Solomon was and always will be the wisest man to have ever lived, and his proverbs provide the proof.

From the book of Proverbs, I was led to the New Testament gospels of Matthew, Mark, Luke, and John and the writings of the apostle Paul. It was in these writings that I found my true "hero" in my Lord and Savior, Jesus Christ. Once again, bringing my life experiences to what I was reading left me in absolute awe of the *man* Jesus was.

As believers, we have a tendency to consider only the deity of Jesus, and we forget that He was a man—a perfect man, but truly a man in every sense. This reality was not lost on me, however, a former made man who once aspired to be a "man's man," as the mob life so emphatically demands.

I was completely drawn to the qualities Jesus possessed in that regard. I saw Him as the ultimate man's man, towering above all those who came before Him and those who would follow. His character was flawless. He was genuine in His humility, never acting as if He was better than those around Him, while knowing that, in fact, He was. In His leadership abilities, He was the antithesis of the men who controlled La Cosa Nostra. What I saw in Jesus made me realize that the mark of a true leader is his ability to lead while controlling his power, not just exerting control over others. Jesus felt no need to flex His muscles as most mob guys do. He was completely comfortable in His skin. His followers were drawn to Him out of love, and His enemies envied Him out of fear of not being loved as He was. Jesus became the personification of my image of a man's man, being totally unique in His character, His mission, and His message.

And what was His mission? To redeem the world from the eternal consequences of sin. The greatest gift a man can give is to lay down his life for another, and Jesus willingly sacrificed Himself for the benefit of all mankind. In doing so, He delivered a message that was crystal-clear: Love God first, and then love your neighbors as you love yourself. Jesus gave the human race a directive and common sense along with the experience of living, and it was clear to me that the world would be a far better place if we were to follow His directive.

In His life, His mission, and His message, Jesus provided the evidence to prove He truly was a man's man in every way. But was He really the Son of God?

In the New Testament gospels, Jesus Himself boldly proclaimed that He is, in fact, the Son of God. "…My father, whom you claim as your God, is the one who glorifies me. Though you do not know Him, I know Him" (John 8:54-55). "If you really knew me, you would know my Father as well" (John 14:7). He went on to proclaim that He was sent by His father in heaven to be the Savior of all mankind, and belief in Him is the only way to enjoy everlasting happiness in heaven. "I am the resurrection and the life.

He who believes in me will live, even though he dies; and whoever lives and believes in me will never die" (John 11:25-26). "For God so loved the world that He gave His one and only Son, that whoever believes in Him shall not perish but have eternal life" (John 3:16).

Jesus left no doubt as to whom He claimed to be, which is how it should be. Anyone proclaiming to be the Son of God should not equivocate. He or she *must* be explicit. In the same regard, I could not equivocate in determining whether to believe in Him or not. Jesus left us no wiggle room, no option for mankind to claim He was a prophet or merely an exceptionally good and moral person. "I am the way and the truth and the life. No one comes to the Father, except through me" (John 14:6). Bottom line: I either believe Him when He proclaims that He is the Son of God and accept that He truly is the Savior of the world, or I do not. There is no provision to "sit on the fence." I am either for Him or against Him.

Consider this: If Jesus was not who He claimed to be, we are left with some very disturbing alternatives as to who He really was. If He knew He was not the Son of God and "one with the Father," then He was a bold-faced *liar*. And if He was a liar, then He was also a *hypocrite*, because He told others to be honest while He was living an outrageous lie. But if Jesus really believed He was the Son of God when, in reality, He was not, then He had to be a *lunatic*. God is either God who knows all things and cannot be mistaken, or He is not. Furthermore, if Jesus was deceitful in deliberately telling others to trust in Him for their eternal destiny when He could not back up His claims, then He was a *demon*, unspeakably evil in leading people astray for all of eternity. And finally, Jesus would have been a colossal fool if He were either a liar or a demon, because it was His claim to deity that led to His brutal and agonizing death by crucifixion.

The very character of Jesus argues persuasively against His being a liar and a con-man and therefore an evil fool. He spoke of truth and virtue at every opportunity. His life exemplified the very message He proclaimed. He left us with the most profound moral instruction and example that anyone has ever given. The very notion that a deceiver, an imposter of such monstrous proportions, can teach such ethical truths and live such a morally exemplary life is absurd and positively beyond belief.

Furthermore, the consistent life and teachings of Jesus made it clear that He was not a lunatic. A lunatic cannot effectively conceal abnormal behavior over the course of his lifetime. Abnormalities and imbalance are part of his lifestyle. When analyzing the life of Jesus, we do not find inconsistent and unbalanced behavior. To the contrary, we see a man who was mentally sound and balanced and very consistent in both His behavior and His message.

The life and teachings of Jesus support the notion that He was neither liar nor lunatic, con-man nor demon. Jesus predicted that He would be crucified for the sins of all mankind. He further proclaimed that He would rise again from the dead and sit at the right hand of His Father in Heaven. In analyzing the life of Jesus, I realized the real truth for Christianity was in the evidence, or lack thereof, supporting His claim that He would rise from the dead. For me, if there was no resurrection of the body of the Messiah, then my belief in Christianity would have been buried in the tomb along with the body of Jesus. I would only surrender my life to a living God and not to a dead man, regardless of how moral He might have been. If Jesus could not save Himself, how could I have faith that He could save me?

Once again, in proclaiming His resurrection from the dead, Jesus left no grey area. He either is the living Son of God, or He is a rotted, decayed corpse. My life in the mob had provided me with a unique perspective to understand the very clear and convincing evidence that proved, beyond any doubt, that Jesus Christ is the risen Son of God and Lord and Savior of the world. I found this overwhelming evidence in examining the lives of His apostles.

These were ordinary men: fishermen, a doctor, even a tax collector. All of them willingly left their trades and accepted the call of the young carpenter to follow Him. Jesus had no organization. He had no prior history or reputation that would have enticed them to follow Him. He did not promise to provide them with wealth or power. In fact, He promised them nothing on earth would be gained by following Him. They were not required to take an oath, to shed their blood, or to swear allegiance under penalty of death. They faced no retribution from Jesus if they did not obey Him. In fact, they were most threatened by those who condemned them for following the young teacher. And yet, they not only chose to follow Him, they chose to follow Him to their deaths.

Most of the original disciples of Jesus suffered violent deaths as a result of their refusal to renounce Him. Philip, for example, was stoned to death. Barnabas was burned at the stake. Peter was crucified upside down. Paul was beheaded, as was Matthew. Andrew was also crucified. Luke was hanged. Thomas was speared to death. Mark was dragged to death. James was beaten and clubbed to death. And John was exiled and left to die on the Isle of Patmos.

These men were not criminals, nor were they bound to any criminal organization. They had committed no wrong against the state. In fact, Jesus had instructed them to obey the laws of the land and even to "give to Caesar what is Caesar's, and to God what is God's" (Matthew 22:21). Each of these men was put to death simply because he believed in Jesus and His message with all of his heart, mind, and soul. Had they simply renounced their allegiance to Jesus, as I had renounced my allegiance to La Cosa Nostra, they would have escaped their horrible fates. There was no indictment hanging over their heads. They faced no jail time. They were not asked to cooperate with the law enforcement officials of their day, nor to give testimony concerning the crimes of their fellow apostles. They just had to renounce Jesus and walk away with their lives. There isn't a mob guy alive that wouldn't take that deal, myself included. Yet, each one of those men had adamantly and boldly refused to deny Jesus. In the face of certain death, not one of them broke rank and agreed to renounce his membership in the family of Jesus Christ. This is powerful evidence to a former mobster.

Even more incredible to me was that their refusal to deny Jesus came when He was no longer with them in the flesh. He wasn't there to protect them or to provide comfort or assurances to them any longer. He was gone! So why would they have taken the position they did? What could have made these men react in a way that flew in the face of any logical or reasonable course of action? The answer is clear: They were convinced beyond any reasonable doubt that Jesus Christ had risen from the dead and truly was the Son of God.

They were convinced by the evidence they had seen with their own eyes, heard with their own ears, and touched with their own hands. In 2 Peter 1:16, the apostle tells us, "We did not follow cleverly invented stories when we told you about the power and coming of our Lord Jesus Christ, but we were eyewitnesses of His majesty." The apostle John quite clearly corroborates Peter's testimony in 1 John 1:1-5 when he speaks of seeing, hearing, and touching the "life" that came down from the Father in heaven. These apostles did not follow Jesus by blind faith, but rather because of hard, cold, factual evidence.

Many of the apostles had witnessed Jesus die a horrible death by crucifixion. Some of them fled on that day, fearing they might meet with the same fate. Three days later, they saw Him again and He was alive, raised from the dead, just as He told them He would be. He remained with them on earth for forty days before they witnessed His ascent into heaven. During that time, it is recorded that over five hundred of His disciples witnessed the resurrected Savior. If that was not true, how else could their dramatic about-face be explained? To me, this was strong, irrefutable evidence of the resurrected Jesus.

Had the apostles been left with the battered and beaten corpse of the crucified carpenter, do you believe they would have "invented" the story of the resurrection, knowing they would be met with extreme retribution by the enemies of Jesus? And why was the crucified corpse of Jesus not placed on full display for all to witness by His enemies? They knew very well that He boldly predicted He would rise again from the grave on the third day after His crucifixion. Jesus was as dangerous a figure to His enemies in that day as Osama Bin Laden would later become for the United States. You can rest assured that if and when Bin Laden is discovered and killed, his body will be on display for all the world to see. His corpse will appear on the cover of every newspaper and magazine and on the screen of every television set in the world, declaring to all that he has been defeated. How often did you see the image of Iraq's fallen dictator, Saddam Hussein, crawling out of that hole in the ground and later hanging by the neck at his gory execution?

Jesus had very powerful enemies who could have ended the "Jesus myth" and proved Him to be an imposter, had they only produced His corpse. I have heard the popular explanations for their failure to do so, that the expert Roman executioners had botched the crucifixion and enabled Jesus to survive, and He somehow recovered and slipped away into oblivion, never to be seen again. Or better yet, His body had been stolen by His apostles and buried in a hidden tomb, so they could invent the resurrection myth that would eventually lead to their own executions.

An honest investigation into either claim will lead any logical person to conclude, as I did, that these excuses should not even be dignified with a response. If Jesus had not risen from the dead, then His most loyal followers would have become bigger informants and turncoats than infamous mob turncoats Sammy "The Bull" Gravano, Joseph Valachi, and Jimmy "The Weasel" Fratianni combined. And they would have had every right to turn on Him; He would have been a bad person. The story of Jesus would be more infamous then that of Al Capone, John Gotti, or even Adolph Hitler. The fact that the apostles remained loyal to Jesus until their deaths is irrefutable evidence, beyond any reasonable doubt, that Jesus Christ is truly the Son of God.

Case closed!

CHAPTER 11:

THE CONFIRMATION

... "You really are the
Son of God!" they exclaimed.

—Matthew 14:33 NLT

SO I WAS ABLE to collect evidence within the text of the Bible that, when analyzed through my life experiences, proved to me beyond a reasonable doubt that Jesus is the Son of God and Savior of the world. And, as it turns out, the entire Bible was written for that singular purpose.

But is the Bible text really reliable? I cannot claim first-hand knowledge of its authenticity, nor have I ever met any of the authors of the various books. I haven't met any of the characters the Bible portrays, and I certainly wasn't an eyewitness to the resurrection of Jesus. If the Bible is not a reliable, credible text, then it's a colossal sham, the product of a major conspiracy created to deceive the human race. And if so, and the authors and transcribers were alive today and living in the United States, they could be indicted under the RICO statute and accused of masterminding a criminal enterprise that engaged in massive fraud and deceit.

Even though the Bible on its own provided me with clear and convincing evidence of the deity of Jesus, I wanted to look for further corroborating evidence. Luckily, while I was in the Hole, Cammy sent me hundreds of books from which I could draw that information. I had enough time on my hands to diligently and carefully read them and, trust me, I did. Furthermore, I was permitted to have a personal CD player with headphones, and I would listen daily to the radio evangelists who were so gifted in interpreting Scripture and were able to provide much of the evidence I was seeking. I will be forever grateful to Pastor Greg Laurie (who just recently I had the absolute pleasure of meeting) for helping to strengthen my faith in Jesus and the reliability of the Bible.

There are many more gifted authors and evangelists who have written scores of books that carefully and convincingly provide the factual evidence corroborating both the Bible's authenticity and the reliability and credibility of its written texts: Lee Strobel (again, who I have had the pleasure of meeting), Josh McDowell, and the ever brilliant C.S. Lewis, to name a few. I encourage you to read the works of these very well-informed and gifted men.

I found out that the Bible stands alone among all other books ever written. The Bible is the only book in existence that remains completely consistent despite its authorship across multiple centuries, continents, languages, authors, and subjects. More copies of the Bible have been produced than any other book in history. No other book in history has been translated, retranslated, and paraphrased more, and it has never diminished in style or correctness, nor has it ever faced extinction.

Plus, to my amazement, I discovered that no unconditional prophecy of the Bible, even those about events up to the present day, has gone unfilled. Not one! And there are hundreds of them, some of them made hundreds of years in advance of their fulfillment. It doesn't matter what type of prediction it was—the Bible presents the good, the bad, and the ugly; the right and wrong; the best and the worst; the hope and despair; and the joy and pain of life.

Civilization has been influenced more by the Judeo-Christian Scriptures than by any other book or series of books in the entire world. All good-faith scientific analysis has rendered the Bible infallible, from archeologists and historians to physicians and biologists. In fact, as the scientific opponents of the Bible attempt to prove it wrong, time eventually proves it right; science, astronomy, and medicine slowly but surely concede to the accuracy of the Scriptures, and many scientific theories once thought to conflict with the Bible have changed to reflect what it said all along.

Most interesting to me was that the life and death of Jesus are rarely, if ever, in dispute. In most cases, it is only the resurrection of Christ that comes under attack, despite the fact that it is reported in the same texts and by the same authors that report on His life and death. His resurrection confirms His deity and holds the world (and this made man) accountable to His teachings. Once the resurrection is accepted as fact, one has no choice but to believe in Him as the Son of God and, therefore, become subject to what He proclaimed about Himself.

Countless books have been written by brilliant Christian apologetic authors. Apologetics is a field of theology that aims to present a rational basis for the faith, defend the faith against objections, and expose the perceived flaws of other world views. These authors provide volumes of evidence in support of the Bible and Christ's deity. I myself have read several of them, and I encourage you to do the same. Many of these authors were confirmed atheists who set out to disprove the Bible texts and to expose Jesus as a fraud and a myth. In the process of their investigation, they became confirmed Christians, staunch believers in the deity of Jesus.

As I collected and processed all the evidence, it finally convinced me that the Bible was reliable and accurate. More significantly, it proved that I could, in fact, trust in Jesus to be my Lord and Savior. From that point, my heart was filled with a desire to know Him better and to develop my relationship with Him, as my wife and mother-in-law had encouraged me to do so many times before. I wanted very much to trust in Him not only for my eternal salvation, but for my worldly well-being. So I did, and to this very day, throughout all of my trials and struggles, He has never let me down.

CHAPTER 12:
THE TRANSFORMATION

*Therefore, if anyone is in Christ,
he is a new creation; the old has
gone, the new has come!*

—2 Corinthians 5:17

I DIDN'T HAVE a clue as to what I was going to do once I was released from prison. I didn't know how I was going to earn a living and provide for my family, and I still had to deal with the boys in Brooklyn for publicly renouncing my former life. The word on the street was not encouraging in that regard.

There were still many questions in my life for which I had no answers. But I had surrendered my life to Jesus, laid my burdens at the foot of the cross, and believed God was now in control of my life. Somehow and in some way, He would work it all out. I was confident He had a plan and purpose for my life and, now that Jesus resided in my heart, He would begin to reveal His plan to me.

It happened even before I emerged from behind the razor-wired fences of the Federal Correctional Institution in Lompoc. After several months of trying to convince the warden to spring me from the Hole and let me take my chances on the yard, he finally agreed. I was required to sign a release, holding the Justice Department harmless if something were to happen to me. (If I were to get killed, my family wouldn't sue.) I gladly signed the release and was sprung from the Hole that same day. I can't tell you how good it felt.

While I had become spiritually healthy and fit during my isolation, I was twenty pounds lighter and a lot paler than before I was locked down. I was determined to get physically fit before I returned home to Cammy and the kids. I was eager to hit the weight room, walk the track, and play some racquetball.

It was a magnificent California day. The track in the yard of Lompoc federal prison was bathed in bright sunshine. I had my Sony Walkman at full blast, and I was moving briskly to the sound of Billy Joel's "River of Dreams." I was determined to walk at least five miles that afternoon. It felt so good just to stretch my legs and see the birds flying overhead.

I had barely traveled a mile when an inmate that I had known came up to me and said, "Hey, Mike, your name is blasting over the loudspeaker. They're calling you to the warden's office." I thought he was joking, but then I heard it too. "Franzese, report to the warden's office."

My heart sank. Being called to the warden's office was never good news, but in my case, it was probably worse than for most guys. I figured the warden had experienced a change of heart, and it was back to the Hole for the remainder of my sentence. Either that, or he got a call from the Justice Department in New York ordering another round of "diesel therapy"—a tactic employed by the Feds in which an inmate is constantly transported either by prison plane or bus to various institutions. It is designed to wear down a prisoner's resolve and break him emotionally. Whatever the case, I knew he wasn't calling me to join him for a cup of coffee or to ask my advice on prison policy. But off I went, fully prepared for the worst.

I walked into the office and was asked to take a seat in the waiting area. I was preparing my plea to remain in the yard when the warden appeared, accompanied by two men in suits. I had been around long enough to recognize these guys, but before I had a chance to say a word, they flashed their badges and introduced themselves as special agents from the FBI. Not good! Even worse, they said they were from FBI headquarters in D.C. Nothing good ever comes to mob guys from Washington D.C.

I had six months left on my sentence. The last thing I wanted was a visit from the FBI. "What do you guys want now?" I asked, not really wanting to hear their response.

"A favor," they replied. They said I wasn't in trouble, nor were they asking me to cooperate against my former associates. They told me that Major League Baseball, the NBA, NFL and the National Hockey League were working together to create an educational "gambling video" that would be shown to all of their players and league personnel. The leagues were becoming very proactive in educating their players about the dangers of gambling and organized crime. The agents challenged me to talk about athletes and gambling on camera. "You claim you're turning your life around," I recall one agent saying. "We are presenting you with an opportunity to prove it." They said the Leagues needed my help, and the FBI would appreciate my cooperation in that regard.

Needless to say, this was the last thing I expected to hear. After exhaling for a full five seconds, I told the agents I would consider their offer and get back with them.

I understood why they approached me. It made perfect sense. During my years on the streets, I had controlled a number of bookmakers, who took action on both professional and collegiate sporting events. And, yes, we took bets from the athletes themselves. Why? Because in the right situation, an athlete was able to provide an edge to the bookie or the bettor that increased their chances of winning. We'd hook an athlete on gambling, get him into debt, then reel him in for the kill. He would be forced to do something to pay his debt, whether he provided information, shaved points, or flat-out performed poorly in a game. It was a reality I was all too familiar with and was quite skilled at implementing.

Many athletes loved to gamble; maybe it was an extension of their competitive nature. But athletes were no better in picking winners or beating the spread than the average Joe. They won some and, if they continued to gamble, they lost more. The trouble came when they lost money they didn't have. Bookmakers give credit, you know, and my guys were more than happy to extend credit to an athlete. I was the guy the players didn't want to meet if they got into debt. Their unpleasant experience would normally occur on a Monday—Black Monday, we called it, the day a losing gambler had to ante up. It was strictly business for the mob when it came to collecting a gambling debt, or any debt for that matter. It didn't matter who you were; you were going to pay one way or another.

And now, the FBI was recruiting me to share my experiences with all of professional sports. And why not? Who better to educate athletes regarding the dangers of organized crime and gambling than a former mob member who once targeted athletes in his gambling operation? It was a no-brainer. If I agreed to participate, the Leagues would have a new weapon in their ongoing battle to prevent gambling from compromising the integrity of their respective sports.

It certainly was an intriguing thought, but I had some concerns about further inciting my former associates. I was already in the mob's dog house. But the street-life was in the past for me, and assisting the FBI in an anti-gambling video would help silence those who doubted my desire to change the course of my life. I decided to give it a shot. Let the cameras roll.

The video was produced by NBA Productions with contributions from all four professional sports leagues. It ended up being a nineteen-minute piece that very effectively detailed the potential dangers of an athlete's involvement with gambling and organized crime. The production crew came into Lompoc and filmed my portion of the video in the visiting room. I pulled no punches in responding to their questions about how organized crime targets athletes and the consequences for an athlete who defaults on a gambling debt. The crew appeared to be very satisfied with the interview and the information I provided.

When it was over, I returned to my prison routine to finish out the remaining five months of my sentence. Little did I realize just how much of an impact that two-hour filming would have on my future. As I reflect on that time in my life, there isn't a doubt in my mind that God was at work, preparing me for His ultimate purpose in my life.

I was released from my second prison term on November 7, 1995. My wife and children were waiting for me as I walked through the gates of FCI Lompoc, a free man at last. I can't begin to describe how exciting it was to see my family running toward me as I made my way outside. We embraced for less than a minute, as I was anxious to get away from prison and back into the real world. We stopped at Wal-Mart on the way to Santa Barbara, and as we roamed the aisles we made plans to spend a few days just getting reacquainted before continuing the rest of our lives as a complete family.

Within two months of my release from prison in 1995, I was contacted again regarding the issue of gambling among professional athletes. But this time, it wasn't the FBI. Kevin Hallinan was the head of security for Major League Baseball. A no-nonsense Irishman and former New York City homicide detective, Hallinan was determined to do everything in his power to prevent another Pete Rose incident from staining the integrity of the game. Kevin told me the video was proving to be very effective. The baseball players who viewed it were responding well to the message, and he needed me to take the issue a step further. "I want you to come and speak to our players," I recall him saying. "Major League Baseball needs you."

Being interviewed for a video was one thing. Standing in front of an entire team of professional ball players was another. Mob guys didn't do that kind of thing. We pleaded our case in a courtroom, when necessary; we spoke our piece at bail and parole hearings. I stood in front of my crew on almost a daily basis at meetings and sit-downs, normally to reprimand them or to settle a dispute among the soldiers. But public speaking? That was a whole other matter. I certainly had my reservations.

But Kevin was persuasive. He said that I would be making a major contribution to baseball if I agreed to come aboard. He compared my speaking to the players to an army capturing the enemy's general and having him reveal his military's war strategy to the troops. There's something about those Irishmen—especially Irish cops. They are as tough and aggressive in enforcing the law as we Italians are in running the streets.

Kevin brought those qualities to his new position, and they served him well. Although I was still somewhat hesitant, Hallinan won me over. I agreed to give it a shot.

After getting the okay from the commissioner of baseball and the Players Association, which I understand was not easy at first, Kevin wasted no time in presenting me to the players. In the spring of 1996, I visited every Major League team during spring training sessions in Arizona and Florida. I addressed all of the players and coaches in their locker rooms. Kevin would introduce me by first playing the video, and at its conclusion with the house lights dimmed, he dramatically revealed to the room full of millionaire athletes and coaches the organized crime figure they just saw in the video. Donning a pair of trademark dark sunglasses, I began my walk to the podium as the lights were gradually raised, and I swear, you could have heard a pin drop in the room. Some of the players later acknowledged that seeing me come in the room scared the heck out of them. I guess you don't lose that gangster swagger too easily. Bottom line, I had their attention.

I went on to tell them, from my own personal experiences, about the dangers an athlete could face if they were to get caught up in a gambling situation, especially if it involved a bookmaker or a gambler associated with organized crime. No doubt, the presentation had a powerful impact. During that year, Kevin had me address a number of Minor League clubs, as well as all the teams' rookies as part of MLB's Rookie Orientation Program. Hallinan even had me address the umpires. After all, no one associated with the game was immune from having a gambling issue, and no one knew that better than me. I was very encouraged at how well the message was received by everyone, and it re-established my credibility. Even so, I didn't expect I would ever address another player in the future. I had no plans to do so.

Turns out, the spring of 1996 was the beginning of what would become a key element of my life's work. I have addressed the MLB rookies every year since the spring of 1996. Soon after addressing the baseball players, I was contacted by Horace Baumer, who was then Chief of Security for the NBA. Horace was also impressed with my portion of the video, and he asked me to address the gambling issue with the NBA rookies in September of that year. Once again, my message was well-received, so I'm now a regular speaker at the NBA's annual Orientation Program.

In 1998, I was contacted by Bill Saum of the National Collegiate Athletic Association, better known as the NCAA. Bill told me the NCAA was very concerned about the gambling issue among its Division I, II and III athletes in all of their colleges. I knew first-hand that they had valid reason to be concerned. Where do you think most pro athletes began to gamble? Within a short period of time, Bill had me at conferences addressing athletic directors, compliance directors, life skills administrators, and coaches from college athletic programs all across the country. It wasn't long before I started receiving calls directly from the athletic departments of Division I, II and III colleges throughout the United States. Since 1998, I have delivered my gambling message to thousands of student athletes in more than three hundred fifty colleges nationwide. In recent years, while continuing my work with the professional and college sports organizations, I have made presentations to athletes, coaches, and personnel with the Association of Tennis Professionals, the American Football Coaches Association, The Fellowship of Christian Athletes, Youth for Christ, and high schools and middle schools throughout the country, and have contributed to countless news and media organizations worldwide concerning the issue of gambling.

Before long, word of the "Mafia Speaker" spread beyond the confines of professional and collegiate sports to business and criminal justice professors. I began addressing students in classrooms throughout the country, sharing with them my knowledge and experiences in both the areas of business and law. Various law enforcement agencies, including the FBI and local police and sheriff's departments, contacted me to speak at their conferences. I found this to be particularly ironic; I was no longer being asked to cooperate with law enforcement against my former associates, but rather just to share my experiences and to give my testimony. One of the most rewarding aspects of my faith today is the fellowship I share with many of those involved in law enforcement who are brothers and sisters in Christ, as well as with those who are of another faith. The Lord certainly does work in mysterious ways at times.

I have always had a heart for our young people, and I am committed to devoting a good amount of time to educating our youth, especially the gang-bangers who have fallen prey to the ways of the street. They need Jesus in their lives more now than ever before. Our youths have so many negative influences at their fingertips in this high-tech age of instant information-sharing. I am grateful that God has given me a platform from which I can impact their lives in a positive way. They'll listen to the mob guy.

But my experience in addressing groups of people was not limited to the secular world. Upon my release from prison and concurrent with the start of my work with athletes, I visited my old and dear friend, Dr. Myron Taylor. Both he and his staff at Westwood Hills Christian Church were so loving and gracious to me and my family while I was away, so I wanted to thank him. I also wanted to share with him my decision to surrender my life to Jesus. Not only was he eager to hear of my spiritual experience in prison, he wanted me to share my "testimony" with the entire church congregation. Again, how ironic—I was now being asked to give testimony in a church rather than in a courthouse.

I made my first presentation to the congregation of Westwood Hills in 1995, and since then I have shared my testimony with hundreds of thousands of people in churches throughout the country, as well as in men's groups, youth groups, and at Christian festivals. I believe the Lord has impacted the lives of many people through the testimony He has given me. There is no question in my mind that God had this plan and purpose for my life. I can see it on the faces, hear it from the mouths, and read it in the e-mails of those people whose hearts He has been able to touch through my testimony.

As of the time of this writing, Cammy and I and the children are all doing well. We have been so very blessed in that regard. I am in full-time ministry, engaged in speaking all over the country and now being called to speak beyond our borders. I have written four books, a feature film is being produced on my life, and there are quite a few television networks interested in developing a series based upon my experiences.

The entertainment business is a fickle one for sure, and nothing is for certain until the checks are written, the cameras roll, and the fat lady sings. But if God intends for it to happen, I believe it will. I have recently made a commitment in my life that everything I do on a professional level must be in furtherance of the purpose of the ministry God has so graciously blessed me with. If it doesn't serve that purpose, God will not honor it, and it will not materialize, and I am fine with that. The Lord has navigated a course for my life that has brought me through some serious struggles and perils, and He has delivered me for one reason and one reason only—to fulfill His purpose, not my own, and I do my best to honor His plan. My constant prayer is for God to allow me to be effective in His ministry and for me not to screw up the opportunity He gave me to get my life right this time.

To Him goes all the honor, praise, and glory for whatever good He has enabled me to accomplish in my life.

CHAPTER 13:
THE FORMULA

For we are God's workmanship,
created in Christ Jesus to do good
works, which God prepared in
advance for us to do.

—Ephesians 2:10

ON OCTOBER 31, 1975, I was "born again" into a dark criminal life. In an ominous ceremony that included the image of a saint burning in my cupped hands, I swore never to betray "omerta" (the code of silence of La Cosa Nostra), and sealed the oath with the shedding of my blood. Tom DiBella, the acting boss of the Colombo crime family, presiding over the bloody, fiery ritual, went on to condemn my soul to hell should I ever violate the oath and betray my mob family. In a matter of minutes, I had set the course for my earthly life and, unbeknownst to me at that time, for my eternal life as well.

The Bible tells us that there most definitely is a life beyond that which exists here on earth, and that it exists in two very distinct locations: God's kingdom of heaven and Satan's forsaken hell. According to Andy Stanley in his book, *How Good is Good Enough*, a survey taken in early 2002 asked people if they believed in heaven and hell. Almost 90 percent of Americans said they believed in heaven as a real place, while only 30 percent believed in hell. And almost nobody who said they believed in hell thought they were going there.

While the Bible does make it clear that we have free will to decide in which eternal location we will ultimately reside, it does not equivocate with respect to either of their existences. There is a heaven, and there is a hell. Jesus Himself spoke of both eternal places several times in all four gospels of the New Testament. I realize now that, by accepting La Cosa Nostra's oath rather than rejecting it, I had effectively condemned myself to hell. For seventeen years of my life, in the absence of a heart filled with Jesus, I lived every day in violation of the laws of God and those of man. For that, I stand convicted.

On November 13, 1991, in a desperate attempt to escape the agonizing pain of a heart drowning in a sea of hopelessness, I fell to my knees and surrendered my life to my Lord and Savior, Jesus Christ. At that moment, the bondage of my past life was broken, the fiery gates of hell were sealed shut, and the gates of heaven were swung open for all eternity. Some might dismiss the belief I have in my salvation as a display of arrogance from a former mobster; I assure you, it is not. My confidence in salvation comes from the knowledge of and trust in God's word, that the sins of even a wretched, unworthy, undeserving former mobster like myself, through the "gift" of God's grace, are washed away in the blood of Christ.

If we confess our sins, he is faithful and just and will forgive us our sins and purify us from all unrighteousness.

—1 John 1:9

"Come now, let us reason together," says the Lord. "Though your sins are like scarlet, they

shall be as white as snow; though they are
red as crimson, they shall be like wool."
—Isaiah 1:18

I believe with all of my mind and heart that my Father in heaven had a plan and purpose for my life different than that of my father on earth, and His plan would ultimately provide for my passage into heaven.

But the plans of the Lord stand firm forever, the
purposes of his heart through all generations.
—Psalm 33:11

It is now time to "cut to the chase." You need to make a decision as to what direction you will take your life, not only for the present, but for all of eternity. It is my hope that, in reading this book, you will realize that you were put on this earth specifically to fulfill God's purpose (and not your own) as part of His plan for your life.

In his hand is the life of every creature and
the breath of all mankind.
—Job 12:10

This is the bottom line to your very existence. It doesn't matter how or at what point in your life you become aware of God's purpose for you, as long as you do. You can discover it at the age of nine or at ninety-nine. Whatever happened before that time and whatever will happen in the future can all be used in fulfillment of God's plan. It doesn't matter if you were as bad a person as the biblical Saul of Tarsus, or the Colombo family capo, Michael Franzese. The blood of Jesus will purify your sins, and a relationship with Jesus will open your mind and heart to hear God's plan for you.

> In him we were also chosen, having been predestined according to the plan of him who works out everything in conformity with the purpose of his will.
> —Ephesians 1:11

I am often asked if my ministry is an attempt to "make up" for the sins of my past. My answer is no. I cannot make up for what I have done in the past; none of us can. There is no turning back the clock on sin—what's done is done. I can only try to do better and to be obedient to God's word in fulfillment of His purpose in my life. Fortunately, salvation is not obtained by balancing good and sinful works on a scale. It is a gift from God through grace.

> For it is by grace you have been saved, through faith—and this not from yourselves, it is the gift of God.
> —Ephesians 2:8

Furthermore, I believe I was called to ministry as part of God's plan for my life, which He revealed to me through the relationship I developed with Jesus. Trust me, I was not perceptive enough on my own to pursue this calling. God alone deserves the credit for whatever good I have been able to accomplish in His service.

For those of you who believe that you are too bad or too unworthy to fulfill God's purpose in your life, I encourage you to use my life as an example of what God will do when even the worst of us allow Him to work in our lives.

> *Trust in the Lord with all your heart and lean not on your own understanding; in all your ways acknowledge him, and he will make your paths straight.*
>
> —Proverbs 3:5-6

This is my absolute favorite verse in the Bible. For all of us who have gone down a path of unrighteousness in our lives, this is the verse by which we should endeavor to live.

I am often asked if I ever feel guilty for the sinful acts of my past. Honestly, I carried guilt around with me for quite some time, and yes, I still have regrets for the sins of my past life. But years ago, a very wise and godly man in whom I confided about my guilt gave me some wonderful counsel. He told me not to allow Satan to remind me of what God had already forgotten. Once I surrendered my life to Jesus, all my sins were forgiven—past, present and future. He told me the devil will use our guilt to separate us from God and therefore prevent us from fulfilling His purpose in our lives. I never forgot those words, and ever since I have not allowed guilt to stand in the way of my ministry and especially in the way of my relationship with Jesus.

> *Blessed is the man whose sin the Lord does not count against him and in whose spirit is no deceit.*
>
> —Psalm 32:2

For those of you who struggle with guilt and believe you are unworthy of God's forgiveness, I encourage you to take comfort in those words, and do not allow the enemy to use guilt to separate you from fulfilling God's purpose in your life. Remember, God sees in us what others may not. Through all of our sins and our often shameful exteriors, God sees our hearts and knows those who belong to Him.

"…God does not judge by external appearance…"

—Galatians 2:6

…The Lord knows those who are his…

—2 Timothy 2:19

I hope my life experiences will encourage you to seek a relationship with our Savior, so that God can reveal His plan and purpose for your life. On the other hand, I would not be surprised if some of you reading this book have come to the conclusion that compared to a former mobster, you are a really good person, and on that basis you are guaranteed a place in heaven. Furthermore, you might conclude that if God had a plan and purpose for a convicted former mobster, He certainly would have a more noble and worthy purpose for a good person such as yourself.

While measured by the world's standards your conclusions might appear logical, God measures our salvation by a different standard. And, like it or not, His standard is the only one that matters. The Bible is abundantly clear on God's standard: "Good" people do not go to heaven—saved people do. Good people do not consummate God's purpose in their lives; only those who accept His Son do. For it is in and through Jesus that we obtain the gift of salvation and that God's plan for all of our lives is revealed.

> *This righteousness from God comes through faith in Jesus Christ to all who believe... For all have sinned and fall short of the glory of God, and are justified freely by his grace through the redemption that came by Jesus Christ.*
> —Romans 3:22-24

In the midst of my life's journey, I discovered what I believe is the formula for all of mankind not only to obtain eternal salvation, but also to experience the fulfillment of God's plan and purpose in their lives. It was revealed to me through a sincere and honest reading of the Bible. I realized that my life on earth all boiled down to my living according to this formula:

ACCEPTANCE & SURRENDER + OBEDIENCE & PREPARATION = FULFILLMENT.

Acceptance of Jesus as our Lord and Savior and the Surrender of our lives to Him;

PLUS

Obedience to God's Word and a period of Preparation for the purpose for which we were born;

EQUALS

Fulfillment of God's plan and purpose for our lives.

That's it! The Bible clearly tells us to first accept Jesus as our Lord and Savior.

> ...If you confess with your mouth, "Jesus is Lord," and believe in your heart that God raised him from the dead, you will be saved.
> —Romans 10:9

Second, you place Him in control of your life.

> I thank Christ Jesus our Lord, who has given me strength, that he considered me faithful, appointing me to his service.
> —1 Timothy 1:12

Third, be obedient to God's voice in your heart.

> "Blessed rather are those who hear the word of God and obey it."
> —Luke 11:28

Fourth, endure the preparation God allows you to experience.

> For it is commendable if a man bears up under the pain of unjust suffering because he is conscious of God.
> —1 Peter 2:19

Finally, you will fulfill His plan and purpose for your life.

> The Lord will fulfill his purpose for me...
> —Psalm 138:8

Notice that this formula does not require you to be perfect. God knows, accepts, and forgives your imperfections. Anyone who believes God expects perfection from Christians has totally missed the message in the Bible. He knows we are sinners and that we will continue to sin, even after Jesus resides in our hearts. He knows we will try to do better and that sin will be less dominant in our lives, but we will still sin. That's why we can never be good enough to earn heaven. Never! For that very reason, Jesus paid the price for all of our sins—past, present, and future—when He gave His life for us on the cross. Never allow your failures in life to separate you from God's love. The wonderful realization I had in the midst of all my struggles is that God wanted me even when I didn't want Him. He wants you, right now, even if you didn't know or want Him before you picked up this book. You will be amazed at the wonders the Lord will provide in your life if you give Him the opportunity to do so.

Also notice that the formula doesn't require you to have a dramatic testimony. Remember the prison guard who simply slipped a Bible into my cell at a time when I was in desperate need of God's Word? He became part of a testimony God is using to touch thousands of lives. God doesn't always place us on a stage or in the limelight, but in no way does it make His purpose in your life any less important than that of the Reverend Billy Graham or of Mother Theresa. The ground at the foot of the cross is truly level. Whether you are rich or poor, famous or a virtual unknown, all those who lay their sins at the foot of the cross are equal in God's eyes. He blesses us according to our individual skills and talents, and He uses them accordingly.

> *Each one should use whatever gift he has received to serve others, faithfully administering God's grace in its various forms.*
> —1 Peter 4:10

It is the quality of your love for Jesus and how He is able to impact the lives of others through you that matters.

I began this book by telling you that it was not by accident that you read beyond its cover. I told you that someone was trying to get your attention. I am sure by now you know, that someone was our Lord and Savior, Jesus Christ.

> *Your eyes saw my unformed body. All the days ordained for me were written in your book before one of them came to be.*
> —Psalm 139:16

I am nothing more then a messenger, delivering the word of God's love through my testimony as a former mobster and converted follower of Jesus Christ. My hope and prayer in writing this book is that I will have been effective in delivering this message to you, and you will now seek to make Jesus the Lord of your life as He is of mine. Allow Him into your heart, so that God may reveal His plan for you and you may go on to fulfill His purpose in your life. And I also pray that others will do the same when they have been impacted by the presence of Jesus in your life. In doing so, you and I together will have fulfilled the command that Jesus Himself gave us when He told us to "Go into all the world and preach the good news to all creation. Whoever believes and is baptized will be saved, but whoever does not believe will be condemned." (Mark 16:15-16)

To put it in street terms, I hope I have made you an offer you can't refuse! With Jesus residing in your heart, your plans will coincide with God's plan and purpose for your life, and they will succeed.

Commit to the Lord whatever you do and your plans will succeed.

—Proverbs 16:3

ACKNOWLEDGMENTS

First and foremost, I want to thank God for giving me a second opportunity to fulfill His plan and purpose in my life. To Him goes all the glory and honor for the work He has so mercifully allowed me to do.

This book would not have been possible without the support and dedication of those mentioned below.

To my Outreach *Family* who have been so supportive of me and all my work. You have contributed above and beyond my expectations in furthering the purpose of the ministry God has entrusted me with.

To Jennifer Dion, my editor and *Boss* at Outreach, for giving me the opportunity to write this book and for not having me *whacked* for all of my missed deadlines.

To Chad Cannon, my *Underboss* at Outreach Events. Your service in fulfilling the purpose of this ministry has been invaluable in every respect. You are the man!

To Esther Federokevich, my *Consigliere* and literary agent, for all of your advice and efforts on my behalf. You're the best!

Had it not been for my family, who provided me with all the motivation needed to walk away from the darkness and into the light, I would have no story to tell.

To my daughters, Tina, Maria, Miquelle, Amanda, and my baby, Julia. You are all a father could ask for and more. I love you all so very much.

To my sons, John and Michael Jr., the Franzese *crew*. You have certainly been my struggle at times, but you are both very gifted young men. My hope and prayer is that you realize God has a plan for you and that you do all you can to fulfill His purpose in your lives.

To my most precious wife, Camille, my partner for life, for being my rock, for keeping me grounded, and for never letting me forget that I am far more blessed than good. I love you, honey, "forever and ever and always."

ABOUT THE AUTHOR

Today, Michael is an author and a highly sought-after speaker who tells his inspiring story to churches, prison and youth ministries, as well as sports organizations like the NBA, MLB, NCAA, and others. He has been featured at corporate events, industry conferences, radio and television programs, and on more than 350 college campuses across the country. His life story of incredible personal transformation leaves audiences on their feet and ready to face their own challenges. Franzese is the author of the autobiographical *Quitting the Mob* and *Blood Covenant*. His most recent release is *I'll Make You An Offer You Can't Refuse*, which features insider business tips that helped Michael make millions (minus the illegal part.) You can find Michael's books online or at your local bookstore.

Michael lives with his beautiful wife Camille and is the father of seven children.

For information about having the author speak to your organization or group, please contact:

Outreach Events

866-400-2036 | events@outreach.com

Visit Michael online at

w w w . m i c h a e l f r a n z e s e . c o m

Also by
Michael Franzese:

Also by
Michael Franzese:

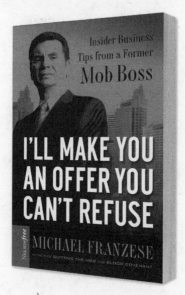

www.michaelfranzese.com